Lois Eger was ⟨ ⟩ and humorous comments could always be expected to be inspiring and insightful. She was a woman of God. Her book, *Pathway to Peace*, contains her best thoughts and insights to a joyful adventuresome life in Christ, which she insists and I agree, are available to everyone.

Dr. Bill Bright, Founder and President
Campus Crusade for Christ International

This inspiring book is part of the wonderful legacy of faith of one of my dearest lifetime friends, Lois Eger. Lois was a rare woman of God, strong in her faith, transparent in her relationships, and she could be either dead serious or hilariously funny depending on the situation. Her great desire was for people to know Christ and the reality of the Spirit-filled life, and only God knows the untold numbers of lives she touched. Through this unique book, with her unusual insights and method of expression, Lois will continue blessing others and drawing them to an intimacy with the Savior, whose glorious presence she now enjoys.

Vonette Z. Bright, Co-founder
Campus Crusade for Christ International

Pathway to Peace

Lois Eger

with Keith Money

LEGACY PUBLISHING

Studio One, 201 Monroe Ave., Maitland, Florida   32751

Published by:
LEGACY PUBLISHING
Studio One, 201 Monroe Avenue
Maitland, Florida 32751

Copyright © 1998 by Legacy Publishing

ISBN 0-9628733-1-4

Scripture quotations designated NAS are from *The New American Standard Bible*, © Lockman Foundation 1960, 1962, 1963, 1968, 1971, 1972, 1975, 1977.

Scripture quotations designated KJV are from the *King James Version* of the Bible.

Printed in Canada.

Dedication

I would like to dedicate this book to my husband, Leroy Eger, who without his encouragement and support this book would never have been written, and also to the staff of Campus Crusade for Christ who felt the call to turn from what the world had to offer, and raise their own support, to take the message of Jesus Christ around the world.

When we were being interviewed to join as associate staff members, I was asked why I felt called to this ministry. My reply was, that I didn't feel called but my husband has a definite call and I asked God to give me the will to follow and He did. So to all the spouses who joined because of the call of another, I also dedicate this book.

Introduction

Now I lay me down to sleep
I pray the Lord my soul to keep
If I should die before I wake
I pray the lord My soul to take

When this does happen and it will - sooner or later -, I'll be taken care of. What a wonderful feeling to know where I will spend eternity.
How blessed my life has been. More than 50 years of marriage to a very talented, wonderful husband who has given me an exciting life, and two loving, interesting daughters and four superior grandchildren and so far one great granddaughter. I've enjoyed life to the fullest, especially the freedom to just be myself.
At 72 I'm no longer pressured to conform with what others think I should be doing or saying (not that I ever did much conforming anyway). It is a great time of life. Seventy years is all we are promised so the way I look at it, the time I have from now on is an added bonus.
I have the opportunity to begin polishing the things I know how to do and to learn new ones.
Now is the time to take a look at my life right now. Am I investing my time and treasures in the things that really matter and will make a difference?
I regret that I have not written more letters and that I have wasted so much time sorting my stuff.
I have also been super blessed with many wonderful friends and a very special town in which to spend the rest of my days on this earth. Although, the way my life has been, there may be many exciting adventures awaiting me in the days to come. It is special to just get up each morning and just see what happens.
My desire is that when God does call me home, my family and friends will have to smile when they think of me and to know that I'm smiling, too. If there are tears, I hope they will have to drop down on a smiling face with happy memories.

(From Lois to her friends and family just a few years ago.)

Table of Contents

Chapter One

"Have you met Lois?"

Chapter 1

L ois Tumblin Eger was an ordinary person, who lived an extraordinary life. Her greatest achieve ments at first glimpse appeared to be admirable but commonplace. She was a faithful loving wife to Leroy Eger for 55 years and a loving and nurturing mother to her daughters, Judy and Kaye.

Lois was a friend, confidant, and teacher to those fortunate enough to know her. Her friends will tell you that she had a sense of humor that brightened the world around her and the honesty to speak the truth when she saw it.

For seventy-eight years she lived a life that to the casual observer was quite ordinary, but it was not. Lois Eger lived an extraordinary life that profoundly affected scores of people she never met.

Lois knew something that many of the great men and women of her generation never learned. She found a life of peace, not the simple absence of daily conflict, but peace that overcame the troubles life brought her way. A peace that often was not understandable to many around her, a peace so profound that its power not only changed one woman, but has the power to change the world.

Lois Tumblin Eger was born on February 6, 1920. Her mother, Winifred West Tumblin, and her father, James Samuel Tumblin, lived on West Street in Tampa, Florida. The third of four daughters, she showed from her earliest days a zest for life, a heart full of joy and a single minded determination of an individual spirit.

She grew up in a home filled with laughter and Christian commitment. Her father was a successful Tampa businessman and her mother was a caring woman with a deep faith in Jesus Christ.

Lois' earliest memories centered on the time she spent at First Baptist Church in Tampa. The church was the center of the family's religious and social life. There was never a time in Lois' life that she was not aware of the presence of God. Her family was committed to Christ and his work.

Lois' mother was a godly woman. She was not only faithful to her church, but spent countless hours ministering to the needy in their community. Lois' father had a big car and one of her earliest memories was going with her mother in the big car to collect eggs from the farms around Tampa. Once they had collected the eggs, they would go door to door selling the eggs to raise money for the Salvation Army's home for unwed mothers. Lois knew from her earliest years that a godly life was a life of service.

Lois was a tomboy who feared nothing. She loved to climb trees and ride her red bicycle. She loved to laugh and was never afraid to tell anyone what was on her mind.

She was not the best student in the family. Her older sisters, Winifred and Katherine, were excellent students and the pride of their teachers. When Lois had the same

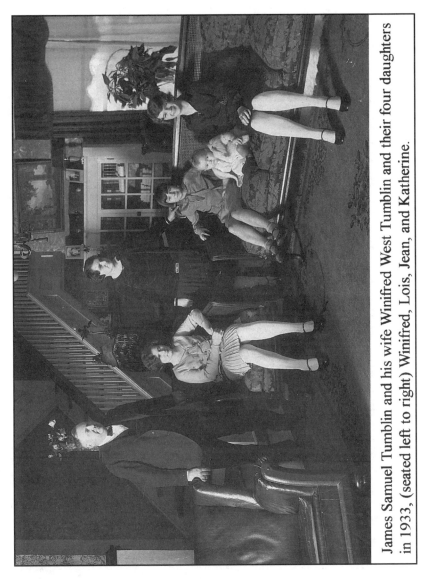

James Samuel Tumblin and his wife Winifred West Tumblin and their four daughters in 1933, (seated left to right) Winifred, Lois, Jean, and Katherine.

teachers, they would often ask, "Are you sure you are Winifred and Katherine's sister?" Lois always felt that people expected her to be like her sisters, but Lois could only be herself. Schoolwork was too serious for a little girl with laughter in her heart. Lois always heard a different drummer, and she did not mind sharing its beat with anyone she met.

Lois' sense of humor was innate. Joy and laughter were as natural to her as drinking water. Whenever Lois met obstacles in life, she always tried to find something to laugh about.

Her love of life made her a popular teenager. Lois was pretty and fun to be around. She turned the heads of many of Tampa's best young men. Her aunt, called "Sister," said, "Boys would just come out of the wood work when Lois was around."

Lois was not afraid to go steady with two boys at once. She found it easy to date one boy from school and another from church. As long as they did not know each other, everything was great. One day, while getting ready for a date with a boy from school, she heard the door bell ring. Her sister Jean came to tell her that her boyfriend from church was waiting in the parlor. As she was talking to Jean, she saw her boyfriend from school pull up outside her house in his car. Jean asked Lois what she was going to do. "How do you handle two boyfriends in one place at the same time?"

With a bounce in her step and a smile on her lips, she went to the parlor. She asked her boyfriend from church to come outside with her. She introduced the two young men and informed them that they all three would spend the evening together. They all three had a great time because Lois would have it no other way.

Lois' memories of high school are more about creative ways to get out of school early on Fridays than about anything she learned. She did well, however, and graduated in the spring of 1938.

After attending business school, Lois went to work at Maas Brothers Department Store in Tampa. She loved working as an assistant to the buyer of the women's

(Clockwise from lower left) Lois, Winifred, Katherine, Jean, and their mother Winifred Tumblin in 1967.

specialty shop. For a while she thought about becoming a fashion buyer, but in the spring of 1942, Lois' life was changed forever.

One Sunday morning as she went to church, she spotted a shiny black Ford convertible. She thought to herself, "That is a nice car." Later that week a friend from church invited her to play tennis. Her friend wanted to introduce her to a young man from Texas.

Leroy Eger, a Texas Tech engineer, from Lubbock, Texas, had come to Tampa to work in the shipyards. He wanted to fly in the Army Air Corps, but his skills were needed in the shipyards. The United States was at war and needed ships fast. Leroy worked seven days a week and had little time to make new friends.

The same Sunday morning Lois spotted the convertible, Leroy met a woman who attended the First Baptist Church. During their conversation, she asked Leroy if he would like to meet any the young women from the church. Leroy said that he would and she invited him to play tennis with her and her husband. She told Leroy that she would find a doubles' partner for him.

Lois thought the idea of playing tennis with a young man from Texas was exciting. The tennis match was less than inspired, but Lois was enchanted by the handsome young Texan. She accepted his invitation for a ride home. When she saw Leroy's car, she realized it was the same shiny black convertible she had seen earlier in the week. Lois would tell a friend later, "I think I have finally found the right convertible."

Lois and Leroy were inseparable over the next few weeks. He would pick Lois up from work and they would be together until Leroy had to report for his job on the "graveyard shift." Lois, who had always been so confident and glib with the young men she had dated, was falling in love.

Lois had always resented young men who became too serious after a few dates. She just wanted to have fun and they wanted to talk about commitment and marriage. Lois told Leroy about this one afternoon as they sat watching the sun set over Tampa Bay. As Lois told Leroy of the several proposals she had turned down, Leroy asked "What would you say if I asked you to marry me?" Lois, who was never without a witty response, paused and said "I don't know what I would say, ...yea ...or uh-huh."

Lois Tumblin married Leroy Eger on Easter Sunday, April 5, 1942. It was a simple ceremony at the

Leroy and Lois Eger shortly after their wedding in 1942.

First Baptist Church of Tampa. The evening was light hearted and happy, just like the bride.

Early married life was exciting, but hard. Lois loved Leroy, but she did not like the house work. She made the best of her domestic chores, (that was Lois' way about everything she encountered), but she never learned to like doing dishes. She gave her all to her marriage and was determined to be the best wife she could be.

In the spring, of 1944, Lois gave birth to her first daughter, Judy. Lois loved being a mother. She would make clothes for Judy's dolls, and have tea parties. She taught her daughter that life should be filled with joy and laughter.

Church did not interest Leroy in their early years of marriage. Lois knew that it was important that she take Judy to church, and she did. Wherever they moved in those early years, Lois would find the First Baptist Church and become involved in its ministry.

It was in these early years of marriage that Lois began to discover a pathway to peace. It was the time she spent alone with God and in the reading of His Word. Life would hold many tough times for Lois, but her strength, joy and peace would find its source in her intimate walk with God.

After the war, the Egers moved to Bartow, Florida. Leroy's grandfather had a small bait company. Leroy helped his grandfather automate the manufacturing process and build a new factory. Before long, Eger Bait Company was the largest bait company in the United States.

Leroy wanted to buy the company from his grandfather, but his offer was not accepted. Disappointed, the Egers moved to Texas. Leroy went to work for his uncles in Lubbock and Fort Worth and quickly helped the construction firm they owned become a major government contractor. The large projects he worked on took the family first to New Mexico and then to Kansas.

In 1950 Kaye was born. Lois was happy. She had two beautiful daughters and a very successful husband. Leroy was providing for all the family's material needs and Lois was learning more each day to trust God for

The Eger family photo in 1954

all the things money could not buy.

Lois missed Florida, the water and the sunsets. In 1955, Leroy finished a major project for the government while the family was living in Wichita, Kansas. Lois took the girls for a visit to see their grandmother Tumblin in Tampa. While she was away, Leroy became gravely ill. Lois returned to Kansas. It was during this illness that Lois realized just how alone their family was, away from friends and families. This was a time of growth for Lois as she learned to depend more and more on God and his promises.

After Leroy's recovery, Lois told Leroy that she wanted the family to move back to Florida. Leroy sold his business interests in Kansas and moved the family to Jacksonville, Florida. Leroy started the business that would become Port-O-Let.

God blessed the Eger family. Leroy's business prospered and Lois continued to grow in the Lord. Leroy began to attend church with Lois and take an active part in the ministry of the church. Leroy thought it would be good for business if he was active in his church. Before long, however, Leroy began to serve because of his love for God and His work.

Lois and Leroy received an invitation to attend a seminar being led by Howard Butts at the Foutainbleu Hotel in Miami Beach. The seminar was concerning Christian growth. It was during this seminar that Lois was confronted with a question that would have a profound impact on her the rest of her life. The speaker at the small seminar asked those attending, "If you are not ready to yield your entire life to God, are you willing to be made willing?"

Lois was not certain what God expected of her. She had lived her entire life loving him and His Word, but she knew He wanted more of her. She prayed, "Lord I am willing to be made willing." She did not know then, but God was preparing to work miracles in the life of the Eger family.

In 1964, Leroy became deathly ill. The doctors did all they could, but eventually came to conclusion there was little hope for his recovery. Lois was not hopeless. Her trust was in God's word and she turned to God for His help. She had a peace that He was in control.

Leroy lay in his hospital bed as the doctor walked from his room. In the silence of the room he began to pray, "Lord, whatever it is you want, I am ready to give it to you." Leroy began to sob, and for a man who did not cry, wept unexplainably for several minutes. Then suddenly the sobbing stopped as suddenly as it had begun. Leroy continued to pray, "Lord, I am ready now to give you my life. I'll even teach a Bible class." Leroy turned his life completely over to God. From that moment he began to get better.

Leroy asked a nurse to hand him the Bible on the nightstand. Lois had left it there. When Leroy opened the Bible, it fell open to a well-marked place. Leroy read the Phillips translation of James 1:1-8. *"When all kinds of trials and temptations crowd into your lives, my brothers...welcome them as friends! Realize that they come to test your faith and to produce in you the quality of endurance...And if, in the process, any of you do not know how to meet any particular problem he has only to ask God...The man who trusts God, but with inward reservations is like a wave of the sea, carried forward by the wind one moment and driven back the next...the life of a man of divided loyalty will reveal instability...."*

Leroy's commitment was genuine, and Lois' prayers were answered. God blessed the business and the fam-

ily. Leroy began to lead a bible study for his employees and to treat his customers and competitors in the way he felt God wanted. It was during these years that the Egers gave away over thirty thousand copies of <u>Good News for Modern Man</u>. Lois had no memories of a life without God. As a little girl she had given her heart and life to Jesus Christ, sitting on the front porch swing at her parents home. As she grew to womanhood, she grew in the grace and knowledge of the Lord. She realized early in the life of her family that she had to trust God. Lois was willing to be made willing, and God blessed her home and her life.

In the late 1960's, Leroy became involved with Campus Crusade for Christ. Lois was supportive of Leroy but was not sure that she wanted to become too involved herself. When Leroy felt that God was leading him to become an associate staff member with Campus Crusade, Lois realized that if God was calling Leroy, then he was calling her as well.

She faithfully supported Leroy's ministry. It was during these early years of their involvement with Campus Crusade that Lois began to learn what she had already been living. Dr. Bill Bright helped her understand the ministry of the Holy Spirit. Lois learned the importance of "breathing spiritually[1]" and as her understanding grew, a ministry began.

The woman, who had always had a heart of laughter and mind with a sharp wit, began to write about what God was doing in her life and what he could do in the lives of others. Her poems, devotional writings, and allegories spoke of the love of God and a pathway to peace.Lois reached a level of Christian maturity attainable by all Christians, but a maturity that few ever realize. This ordinary woman learned how to live life in

Lois in the early 1960's.

an extraordinary way. She found a pathway to peace. She knew the Peace of God (Philippians 4:7). She learned to be content under all circumstances (Philippians 4:11). She knew with a certainty God was her true source of strength (Phillipians 4:13). She did not worry about what had passed, but trusted the future to God (Phillipians 3:13,14). She knew that all things in her life worked to the good of the life God had called her to (Romans 8:28). Lois lived a full life, a life of joy, love, peace, patience, kindness, goodness, faithfulness, gentleness, self-control (Galatians 5:22,23) and laughter, an extraordinary life.

[1] Please read the pamphlet "Keys for Dynamic Living" available from Campus Crusade for Christ.

A Poet

I try to be a poet
It takes a lot of time
And what I write turns out to be
Some silly little rhyme.

Some verses come real easy
I write them on the double
I haven't made much money
But it keeps me out of trouble.

Chapter Two

Odes and Observations

Chapter Two

Please, Let Me Be Free

What does it mean to be free? Does it mean doing it my way? Don't take away my freedom. I just want to be free. What that really means is that I want to do it my way.

A girl I knew who had difficulty getting along with people wherever she went inspired this verse.

> She has problems
> We all agree
> Adjusting to society
>
> My situation differs
> You can plainly see
> It's society that has the problem
> Adjusting to me.

Do I not have problems with other people? Is freedom the cause of me wanting society to adjust to me or is it just a self-centeredness?

Do I want to be the captain without the responsibility of the ship? Is "Let's do it my way" music to my ears? I don't want to conform because I like being a non-conformist. Although, I do not like it when I find I am conforming to other non-conformists.

When I learned to fly an airplane, it was great. I could go higher or sideways, turn around and even fly upside down if I wanted to (which, of course I never did).

I felt really free until the tower started telling me what to do. Why I wasn't free at all. I was bound by all of their rules.

I had to wait my turn to take off and follow instructions to turn this way or that way, and I even had to get permission to land.

But if I could get out of the control area, I could do just what I wanted to. That is until I came close to another airport and they told me what I could and could not do.

There is much talk about culture shock. After we returned from living out of the country for six months, I was asked how I handled the culture shock. I said, "Oh, I just waited and they got over it." That was supposed to be a humorous retort, but asking the question did help me to realize that I really did not have culture shock. If the people over there had it, I never knew so I guess they got over it.

The Eger's pressurized Cessna Skymaster used in videotaping Christian speakers for the National Institute for Biblical Studies in late 1970's.

Touch And Go's

"Would you like to learn to fly?"
"Yes, I would." was my reply.
"Then read that big red book
And look at the video.
They will inform you of
The things you need to know."

To safely take off and return
I found there was a lot to learn.

To avoid frustration
Make preparation

To be assured, not to fall
Learn recovery from a stall

Stay out of fog
Keep a current log

By experience, I also found
The steering wheel's no good on the ground

All this information, I did apply
As I began learning how to fly

After much practice it happened
A fact I'd always known
The instructor got out and said,
"You're ready to go it, all alone."

Straight down the runway - stay on that line
The responsibility is all mine
Full power - leave the ground
At 500 feet - look around

Still in a climb - start the turn
I do believe I'm beginning to learn!
800 feet will be just fine
Now it's time to start my decline

Well, here I am, flying high
Way up here in the sky
It really is a lovely view
But I know what I have to do
There is no way to get my foot on ground
Unless I bring this airplane down

Downwind is always parallel
In the opposite direction
I really must remember this
To pass the inspection

Carb heat on - cut the power back
Watch that angle of attack
10 degrees flap - now turn on base
This will help slow the pace

At 70 knots, establish a glide
Watch that heading - not too wide
Turn on final - head for the ground
If there is any doubt then go around

Come to level flight - start to sink
It looks okay, I really think
Hold it off - all the way down
Until the wheels are on the ground
The center of gravity moves around
According to balance and weight
But disregarding the limits
May decide my fate

The datum line is stationary
Even though it is imaginary
Moment is weight - times the arm
Checking limits avoids harm

Sometimes the weather is difficult
It will be in a nasty mood
If the cold front caught the warm one
And caused it to occlude

But if all sides are quite equal
And neither side contrary
The front will be no problem
For it will be quite stationary

This will not be the case
If the clouds are cumulonimbus
Stay far away from them
They can be extremely hazardous

If I ever find I'm in a mess
I must call the tower and confess
They'll communicate their judgment
On this I can rely
The only thing I need to do
Is to climb and to comply

If my radio gets sick and dies
I must signal the tower to let them know
Then be sorry I didn't stay on the ground
And been happy with the status-quo.

Our Grandson

Our two year old grandson saw me push a button on the refrigerator door and get a glass of cold water. He walked over and pushed the button without putting a glass under it. Of course, the water squirted on him. It startled him so he started to dodge. First, it hit him in the face, then his left shoulder and his right shoulder.

This situation called for some outside help. He needed to be dried off and the water needed to be mopped up but first and most important of all was to get his finger off the water button.

He was so busy with the immediate problem that he did not recognize the obvious solution.

As an onlooker, it was very clear to me what needed to be done.

We often become so involved with our own problems that we can't see the obvious solution. In his case I was able to physically remove his finger from the button. But that is very unlikely with an adult. An outsider can point out the cause of the problem but ultimately, we have to remove our own finger from the button.

I'm not holding my finger on the button of a critical spirit as consistently as I did for many years but I still give it a push now and then. I always referred to it as "being good at sizing up the situation".

If we could get our finger off the button of self-centeredness, it would be amazing how many of our problems would clear up. A friend shared her anxiety of associating with wealthy people. "What concerns you, their feelings or yours?" Without hesitation she answered, "How I am going to feel?"

"Isn't that a form of self-centeredness?" I asked. Her reply was that even though she had not thought of it like that, she could see how that could be right.

Wasn't that great? In just a few minutes I had solved her problem.

No, she did not get over her anxiety of associating with wealthy people. She was just upset with me. Self-centeredness comes in many shapes and sizes and can cause all kind of problems. It can even cause us to be dishonest.

If we are overly concerned about what others think of us, we have a tendency to do whatever is necessary to make 'us' look good. The truth may have to be slightly twisted and even withheld in part. Looking for some-one to blame for our actions and not admitting to wrong doing causes many problems.

Talk to God

Talk to God, they say
Tell Him all your woes
But why should I bother Him
With something He already knows?

Cleaning Up

Lord, clean the window of my soul
Of all that's dark and dreary
But please don't make me look inside
So much to do would make me weary.

Grace

If you're living by law
Instead of by grace
You won't be smiling inside
Just on your face.

Missed

I missed the meeting at the church
Which was not the thing to do
But from what I heard, evidently
God must have missed it too.

Babe

I'm still on milk, have not matured
This fact must be endured
But if I'm such a babe as I've been told
Why do you think I look so old?

Inspiration

I go to church for inspiration
But much to my consternation
I see one friend with a brand new hat
I notice another is getting fat
I do so hope on judgement day
My mind won't be so far away
If I am doing much the same
I may not hear them call my name.

My Mind

When I read God's Word
It is with delight
Until I find my mind
Has wandered out of sight.

Fire

I'll never catch the world on fire
It is very plain to see
Unless somebody's bush caught fire
Just standing next to me.

Busy

I've taken many courses
To learn of this or that
I even took a six weeks course
To learn to make a hat
I tried to learn ceramics
I did learn how to sew
But I'm so busy taking courses
I've no time to do them though.

When we were being interviewed to join Campus Crusade for Christ as associate staff members, I was asked why I felt called to this ministry. My reply was that I didn't feel called, but my husband has a definite call and I asked God to give me the will to follow and He did.

I was not as teachable as Leroy was and after taking the three weeks' staff training, I penned this poem.

Training with Campus Crusade

You have a language all your own
It starts out with, "Who's on the throne?"
You must be aware there is danger
What this could mean to a total stranger

How many times did I hear it
"Are you walking in the spirit?"
If overheard you'd sound kooky
You must admit, it does sound spooky

I learned from you I had much to do
I must be charming with proper dress
And also remember to always confess
I should aim to claim and declare to share
Discussing jets, I must refrain
Instead, I must explain the train

If you'll check me over you will see
I've learned it all from A to Z
Much information I've stored in my head
Rules and laws galore
But the thing I can't seem to remember
What am I available for?

There sure is a lot of talk going around about the last days from the Christian media. The regular news does not mention it. I don't think they know anything about it. I wonder what it will be like on that very last day. Do you think it could happen like this?

<u>"This is how it will be at the end of the age. The angels will come and separate the wicked from the righteous."</u> Matt 13:49 (TLB)

The Happening

"Wasn't that explosion awful? Are you O-K?"

"Yeah, how about you?"

"I got burned a bit; not bad, though."

"There sure are a lot of people here. What is this place?"

"I think I know, but am not sure. Do you see anyone you recognize?"

"Some look familiar."

"People sure are dressed funny. It looks like a `come as you are' party. What were you doing when it happened.?"

"I was in bed."

"I thought your shirt looked like a pajama top."

"Yeah, it is. Were you in swimming?"

"No, I was doing my exercises. I always wear my bathing suit when I exercise. I still can't believe it really happened, even though I knew it was going to, some day."

"You did? How did you know?"

"I read about it. But, I sure wasn't expecting it to happen today."

"Was it in the newspaper?"

"No, in the Bible."

"I never read the Bible."

"I don't read it much, either."

"Look at those big gates. Ever see anything like that before?"

"There is somebody coming out of a little door over to the side. I can't tell if it is a man or a woman with that long white robe on. It's probably a man."

"Let's get close so we can see better. Those gates have a sign over them. It looks like it says `Believers'. I wonder what that means."

"I know what it means. I'm a believer."

"Believer of what? That this was going to happen. How could you go through something like this and not believe it? I'm a believer too, now."

"That doesn't count. You had to believe before it happened."

"How could you believe before it happened?"

"I'll tell you later. It's too late to do anything about it now anyway. Do you see those young men over there? They were put in jail after they got caught breaking into a house. The man in the white robe is talking to them. Look, he's letting one go through the gate. He probably became a believer while he was in jail. The other two are still standing there. They didn't get to go in. See that big man step up to the gate keeper. Be quiet so I can hear."

"We are officers of the law. Which gate do we go in?"

"Did you see that?" The man in the white robe did not answer him. He just motioned for them to step aside. The officer is saying something else."

"Didn't you understand what I said? We are crime fighters, officers of the law. Would you please let us through?"

My friend said, "I don't want to hear about those men. I want to know what you meant by `It's too late'. Are you saying that I can't get in? How come you didn't tell me about this? I thought we were friends."

"I didn't think you'd be interested."

"If I had known this was going to happen, I would have been. Why didn't you tell me?"

"I should have told you. I wasn't expecting it to happen so soon. I'm really sorry I didn't tell you."

"You're not half as sorry as I am. This is the worst thing that has ever happened to me. What am I going to do?"

"I don't know anything you can do about it now. I have to go over near the gate so I will hear when my name is called. I sure do feel bad about not telling you."

This story is part truth - part fantasy. The truth is that some day we will all face our Maker. Not necessarily at the same time, but we will all come to a day of judgment.

Whether we lived a good life or a bad life won't be the issue. We will not even be judged by which side of the law we were on; only if we are believers or non-believers. The Bible says to believe on the Lord Jesus Christ and you will be saved.

It is true that many times believers do not tell, even their good friends about this. Why? For a number of reasons.

They do not want their friends to think they are religious; or they do not want to be rejected; or they just don't bother to tell them.

THAT IS THE TRUTH - THE REST IS JUST PURE FANTASY.

You really do have to believe before it happens.

THAT PART IS ALSO THE TRUTH.

"There is no eternal doom awaiting those who trust Him to save them. But those who don't trust Him have already been tried and condemned for not believing in the only Son of God."
John 3:18 (TLB)

Preachy

It causes me to moan and groan
When he uses a voice not his own
He sounds so preachy
He doesn't reach me.

Praying

Father in Heaven, you pray
Hear my humble prayer, you say
Then you proceed to express your views
And give out with a bit of news
A change of program you will note
Or mention how we ought to vote
God and I both know, you see
You're not talking to Him
You're just talking to me.

Meditating

I came to hear a sermon
That would help me be much better
But the sermon he is preaching
I agree with to the letter

So don't think I am sleeping
If you look my way
I'm only meditating
In a very sleepy way.

Bearing It

Christians will always
Be winning by sharing it
Unless, of course, they're just
Grinning and bearing it.

Candle

Burning my candle at both ends
Will never give me a fit
My only problem will always be
Just getting one end lit.

So Busy

I joined a garden circle
To learn to make things grow
It was such a busy group
And did put me in the know
To be an active member
I surely did try
But I stayed so busy with it
I let all my flowers die.

Living

I'm thankful for the word of God
I read it every day
Wouldn't it be wonderful
If I could live that way?

God's Business

When I'm running God's business
I often find
It would be much better
If He would just run mine.

Free Advice

My neighbor is so good and kind
A better neighbor you'll never find
I'd like her more and think it nice
If she'd stop giving me advice.

So You Lost Your Joy?

Dear Friend,

I was so sorry to hear of your loss. The same thing happened to me last week. I too lost my joy.

At least that is what I thought until I found out it was not lost, but had been stolen. Can you believe someone would actually steal another person's joy?

Well it happened, and I found out who did it. I knew about this guy because I have had trouble with him lots of times. He must live near by, because he is always hanging around my house, trying to get in.

He lies and steals and is not someone I want around, mainly because he cannot be trusted.

I found out that he had taken my joy when I caught him in my house, trying to get out the door with my peace.

"You put that down," I demanded. "How did you get in.? I thought the doors were locked and bolted to keep you out."

"Well, they weren't. One door was not quite closed and I just walked in." It must have happened when I came in the house with my arms full of packages. Those large bags of frustration I was bringing in from the car probably caused me to be careless about locking and bolting the door.

"Did you steal my joy?" I asked.

"No ma'am, I did not?" he said.

"Yes you did! Now you bring it right back. That was a gift to me from God, and I want it back, now. Is that clear?"

"O K, O K, I'll bring it back. Now get off my back."

"I'll get off your back when you leave me alone. You

have no right to even be in here, and I want you out, now."

"Knock it off, lady. I'm leaving."

"Good", I said and meant it.

I hope that sharing my experience might help you get back your joy, because it was probably stolen, too. We should not have to take a lot of abuse from any thief because: <u>"Greater is He who is in you than he who is in the world."</u>   I John 4:4B (NAS)

It would be nice if we did not have to always be so careful and could just get rid of that guy for good, but I don't know how to do that. I don't want to take a chance of him slipping in again so I'm keeping my doors locked and bolted from now on. I suggest you do the same.

Do let me know if you find your joy. By the way, is your peace missing, also? If it is, I hope you find it soon.

Jesus said, <u>"The thief comes only to steal, and kill and destroy; I came that they might have life and might have it abundantly."</u> John 10:10 (NAS)

Making New Friends

To make new friends, I've found out
Ask them something they know about
People are eager to give information
Making new friends is a nice avocation.

My Dearest Friend

She was only an acquaintance
The day I stopped in for tea
But I wish you could have heard
The nice things she said to me

The nicest thing that I recall
Was that I didn't look thirty at all
For her to say I had style and beauty
Was way beyond the call of duty

After tea was over
On this you can depend
I now consider her
My very dearest friend.

Chapter Three

For Better or For Worse

Dinner At Home?

To cook is one thing I adore
I collect recipes galore
I can put on a stew, and be on my way
While it slow cooks, the live long day
If I dash in, no cause to worry
I can microwave something,
It'll be done in a hurry.

Cooking is easy, no chance of a blunder
But my husband does say,
He has cause to wonder
If all this be true, without a doubt
Why are we always eating out?

Chapter Three

We frequently eat out but that night I decided to cook. I had turned over a new leaf and was planning to change my ways. But it was late when I decided to cook, so it had to be something I could whip up in a hurry.

If I made the cake first it could bake while I was preparing the rest of the meal.

You will not believe what happened. One of the eggs on the counter started to roll. I saw it approaching the edge - tried to catch it - missed. Next impulse was to catch it with my knee.

What a mess. Egg running down the cabinet front and my knee. I wonder why I did that. It was a reflex action; just did it without thinking.

It was not a case of 'I didn't know the gun was loaded'.

I had all the facts. I was well acquainted with an egg, that thick yellow center surrounded by a clear slimy substance and enclosed in a very fragile, usually white, outer casing. Excuse me a minute while I get this mess cleaned up and try to figure out if there is anything I can learn from this disaster. One thing I see right off is that although I realize it was a mistake and I am sorry, it is still up to me to clean up the mess. Being sorry does not make it go away.

I also have a choice. I can make the best of a bad situation or I can let it ruin my whole day.

> I do a lot of foolish things
> At times, I don't act wise
> But I try to think of my mistakes
> As blessings in disguise.

Paul told the Philippians that he was not perfect either and they should try to make the best of a bad situation like he does.

Maybe that is what I should do. He told the Galations that unless we let God's Spirit tell us what to do, we all just naturally do the wrong thing sometimes.

In all the excitement, I have misplaced my sandals of peace. They must be around here someplace but I don't know where. I wish I could find them.

Do you know how to get egg off a rug?

> Open my eyes that I may see
> The wonderful things in store for me
> Not what will come later along my way
> But the blessings You have for me today.

Improper Navigation

She dashed out at six o'clock
Running round and round the block
He came out in his running suit
And seemed to be in hot pursuit
But due to improper navigation
The refrigerator was his destination.

Lost

I am always losing things
My billfold, my keys, my ring
What you hear is not a rumor
Now I've lost my sense of humor.

Charge Accounts

Charge accounts are very handy
To buy what I want is just dandy
But it does put me in a stew
When my husband finds them overdue.

Are you sure God has called you to be a Proverbs 31 woman?

"There must be more to living than starting each day wondering how I can possibly get the house cleaned, laundry done, and complete the unfinished projects that need attention."

My friend greeted me with this statement when I stopped by her house with some food and clothing. Her club was collecting for the homeless and she was in charge of the distribution.

"What smells so good?" I asked.

"Cookies for my daughter's class," she replied as she rushed to get them out of the oven before they burned. "Sit down, if you can find an empty chair, and I'll join you as soon as I get this other pan of cookies in the oven."

I moved a pile of clean laundry that needed to be folded from the chair to the table and sat down.

"No wonder you are discouraged with all the projects you have in progress. Are you trying to be a Proverbs 31 woman? I see you have a copy of it on your refrigerator door."

"Shouldn't everyone?" she replied. "Isn't she the pattern of a godly woman? I don't know how she managed, but if she could do it, then I should be able to, also. That is my goal."

I had heard many motivational talks on this virtuous woman and wished I could be like her. Then I too could do many other things besides being just a wife and mother; feed the hungry, get the street people places to live, stamp out pornography, clean up television and straighten out Washington. I also would find more time to write and speak.

After I had spoken in a seminar and used the Proverbs 31 woman as an example, a pastor's wife startled me with this statement.

"You know there is no Proverbs 31 woman. She is an imaginary person King Lemuel's mother thought up as the kind of wife her son needed."

Even though I had read the passage many times, this fact had not registered. I always hurried through the first nine verses to the good part about the virtuous woman. The many speakers who presented her as the ideal pattern for a wife had never mentioned she was not a real person.

I reread the passage more closely and that is exactly what it said in verse 1. "These are the wise sayings of King Lemuel of Massa taught to him at his mother's knee." (TLB)

The next eight verses then list instructions for him to follow.

"Does your husband try to be a Proverbs 31 man?"

"I have not heard of a Proverbs 31 man. Is there one?"

"No one has ever mentioned a Proverbs 31 man to me either. In the first nine verses, the king's mother told him how a Godly man should act. She advised him not to spend his time with women because they could be his downfall then she added, unless he could find a woman with all of the qualities listed in verses 10-31.

"It appears you are unsuccessfully trying to live up to an imaginary woman. It is good that your husband did not follow the advice about staying away from women, isn't it?"

"You are right. If he had been trying to be a Proverbs 31 man, he would not have married me, would he?"

"Can you imagine what life would have been like for King Lemuel if he had been able to find a woman like the one his mother thought he needed. It might have gone something like this."

"Mama, I want to talk to you about this wife that you found for me."

"Sure Lemuel, we can talk now, if you like. Your wife is really incredible, don't you think?"

"Busy would be a better word, Mama. She has so many projects going I hardly ever see her and when she is home there is always someone around wanting her advice or help."

"I'm trying to do my job and be a good king, but it is really hard when I am so tired all the time."

"Yes Lemuel, you have been looking rather tired lately. Are you sleeping well at night?"

"I try to, Mama, but she keeps the light burning all night and then gets up before daylight and starts cooking. Another thing, when I come to our quarters after a hard day of making decisions and running the country, I cannot even find a comfortable place to sit. Every chair is filled with her projects: weaving, sewing, and belt-making. She is busy, Mama, real busy."

"I understand what you are saying, Lemuel. She does sound like she may have too much going on at one time."

"What I wanted to talk to you about is her latest project. You know she sells to the tradesmen, so she has money of her own. Yesterday she told me she had bought a field and was planning to plant a vineyard. I asked her who was going to do the planting and she said she was.

"Mama, do you think it would proper for the king's wife to be planting a field? I told her it would be agree-

able with me if she wanted to do a little gardening behind the castle where no one could see her. She has
her mind set on planting that field herself and there is
no way to talk her out of it. She really has a mind of
her own."

"I can see that a problem is beginning to develop,
Son. I will talk to her."

"Thanks Mom, I knew I could count on you. Would
you also tell her to stop suggesting I go sit at the gate
with the men every night? I prefer to come home where
I have a comfortable place to prop my feet up and just
relax. It would be pleasant if she would just sit down
with me. I would enjoy that."

For several years this imaginary scene had been in
my mind, but I kept putting it aside. It was scripture
and since I believe every word of the Bible was written
by men inspired by God, I did not want to be disre-
spectful of anything in the Word of God.

However, it became clear to me that the emphasis
was being put on the many activities of the Proverb 31
woman instead of on her spiritual qualities.

I had been impressed with her busyness and wanted
to be like her in this respect. Other women I met felt
the same way as I did. Another young wife I visited
with had so many worthwhile projects in progress that
her home was suffering. She was so busy with outside
interest that there was very little time left over for her
family.

When a pastor's wife came to me in tears because
she felt so pressured, I learned she had the Proverbs
31 passage taped to her refrigerator. I suggested she
replace it with a more fitting verse that would better
meet her needs. John 15:4. Jesus says, "Abide in Me,
and I in you. As the branch cannot bear fruit of itself,

unless it abides in the vine, so neither can you unless
you abide in Me." (NAS)

All of my efforts at being a godly woman are futile if
I am not abiding.

There are many qualities of this imaginary person
that a godly woman should have, but to hold up her
numerous activities as a guide is misusing the Scriptures.

In verse 30, the summary of what makes her price
"far above rubies" mentions only her spiritual life, not
her outside interest.

Busyness is a tool Satan uses. We can become so
busy we do not take time to pray or read and meditate
on God's Word. "Be still and know that I am God," will
not be operating in our life. Who can be still when there
is so much going on?

When Satan quoted scripture to Jesus, he did not
misquote it. He misused it in a situation where it did
not apply. In my opinion Proverbs 31 has been misused in the lives of many young wives who are trying to
please the Lord by being some super woman when she
should be putting her efforts in learning to abide.

In the first 10 verses of the 15th chapter of John,
"abide" is mentioned 9 times. For Jesus to repeat it
that many times it must be very important. "Abide in
Me: abide in My love: abide in God's love."

He also tells us if we keep His commandments, we
will abide in His love. Then He gives an illustration of
what He expects of us. "This is my commandment, that
you love one another, just as I have loved you."

This is only one commandment and there are many
more to learn as we spend time in the Word of God.

A godly woman does not become so busy she does
not take the time to spend with God and His Word.

I am not suggesting she should be lazy. Slothfulness is mentioned at least 15 times in the Bible and there is not one verse in favor of it. I have not found any scriptures that approve of idleness either.

A young pastor's wife said, "I realized I was living by the law. I saw my high achievement attitude stemmed from a lack of self esteem, as if I had to perform to earn God's love. Galatians 5:1 helped me to understand my freedom in Christ. I am no longer under the law. God loves me for what I am and not for what I do. I am free from performing to meet someone else's expectations."

She found peace and fulfillment as she began learning to rest in the Lord and could stay at home with her two year old daughter without feeling guilty. Caring for her child and her home became a rewarding job. She still teaches a Sunday school class and ministers to individuals when there is a need but her emphasis has changed. She no longer feels pressured to perform. She has been learning to abide.

The Proverbs 31 woman has been used as an example to motivate women to get moving, but many of us are already motivated. I am too busy now, almost fragmented, trying to balance all of the projects with my responsibilities at home. At times, I am not doing a good job at any of it because there is more than I can comfortably manage.

Jesus said not to be anxious for tomorrow. He also said to come to Him when I'm weary and He will give me rest.

If all of my projects are making me anxious and weary, maybe I have too much going on and should reconsider how I'm spending my time and why I am spending it that way.

The Bible is full of scriptures that apply to me so it does not seem wise to disregard all of these and try to be a super woman. That is not my calling from God.

Now, if He does give me a super woman job (and He does sometimes), He will give me the strength I need to do it.

It is very important that I spend time with Him, seek His counsel and practice listening with a willingness to obey.

Has God called me to be a Proverb 31 woman?

My call may not be to bring food from afar, buy a field and plant it or keep the light burning all night but verse 30 applies to all of us.

"Charm is deceitful and beauty is vain, but a woman who fears the Lord, she shall be praised." (NAS)

As I left my friend, I suggested John 15:4 as a more fitting scripture for her refrigerator door, also.

"Abide in Me, and I in you. As the branch cannot bear fruit of itself, unless it abides in the vine, so neither can you unless you abide in Me." (NAS)

All of our efforts at being Godly women are futile if we are not abiding in the vine.

Happiness

You don't find happiness
It finds you
If you trust God to show you
What you should do.

The Fancy Party

I had decided to be very good
And act the way I knew I should
Things went quite well, I must confess
But I did feel quite colorless
I thought before I spoke
Just paused and took a breath
I don't know how the others felt
But I BORED myself to death
I made a real discovery
That will keep me from constraining
I don't 'play the fool' for other folks
It's me I'm entertaining
When a friendship wears thin?

Learning to Drive

Suddenly, I'm aware
Of danger lurking everywhere
I am so happy just to be alive
Since my teenager learned to drive

Taking the Floor

I asked to have the floor
I wanted to be heard
Imagine how embarrassed I was
When I mispronounced a word.

Guests

Having guests is such a pleasure
But the only part I mind
Is having to return
The things they leave behind.

Fast Boat

We have a boat, I like to ride
My husband likes me by his side
He goes so fast around the bend
So he can hurry back again
I like to glide, to take it slow
We can't agree how fast to go.

Disappointed

I hurried back just to see
If you had come home to me
I was disappointed, goodness knows
When all I found were your dirty clothes.

Hurt

My husband is a nice sweet fellow
His disposition is mild and mellow
The only time it isn't so
Is just the time I'm feeling low.
If I wake up feeling sad
He barks at me, he thinks I'm mad
The time I need him most, you see
He really is no help to me.

Your Light

Lord, turn off the dark
That I may find my way
It's the presence of Your light
That will turn my night into day.

He Hurt My Feelings And He Doesn't Even Know It

"Isn't that unbelievable that he could be so insensitive and not know he hurt my feelings? I don't think I will even mention it to him."

That is a wise decision. Don't mention it to your mother, either because after you have it all worked out, it may still be a problem to her.

Men just do that sometimes. I don't know why, but they all do it. Well, maybe not all, but the ones who are married to my friends are guilty, some more often than others.

Once when that happened to me, I was so upset that I could not think of anything else but those unkind words. They occupied so much of my mind they blotted out all of the nice things he had ever said to me, the nice things he had done for me, and the happy times we had shared. They were all momentarily forced out of my mind because the hurt needed room to grow. I fed it with self-pity and watered it with my tears. Receiving so much tender care did make the hurt grow very rapidly.

I was even more upset at him when he didn't even notice how much I was suffering. The situation was now worse than it had been in the beginning. "What am I going to do?" I wondered.

I know, I'll pray for him to change. Speaking to me like that certainly is not honoring to the Lord.

Proverbs 14:1 says,
"A wise woman builds her house, while a foolish woman tears hers down by her own efforts." (TLB)

Maybe I'm praying for the wrong person to change.

In Philippians I read:

"<u>Fix your thoughts on what is true and good and right.
Think about things that are pure and lovely and dwell
on the fine good things in others. Think about all you
can praise God for and be glad about it.</u>" Phil 4:8 (TLB)

I began to realize that in this situation I am only
responsible for my reactions and not his actions.

My peace comes from God and when I lose it, I have
a spiritual problem that needs my close attention.

"Heavenly Father, forgive me for not fixing my
thoughts on what is true and good and right. Fill me
with Your Holy Spirit so that I may be a wise woman
who builds her house and not one who tears it down."

Spring

Spring is here, I should be glad
But so much to do makes me sad
I look around, all that yard
To keep it nice is very hard

I could take an apartment
Or maybe just a room
I always change my mind, though
When my flowers start to bloom.

Bragging

It is nice to brag about her meals
But that does not help the way she feels
The thing she would most like to hear
I could not live without you, dear.

Special Gift

It's your wife's birthday and you want a gift
Something that will really give her a lift
It can't be a gift that costs a lot
Because your finances are in a spot

I have some good advice for you
Just a few things that you could do
Give her a hand when her work's behind
And help her make the children mind

Would she be surprised to hear you say
I very much like your hair that way
Or I can't believe you are twenty-nine
Nineteen would be much more in line?

It doesn't matter how much you spend
Most any gift will do
But let her know the thoughts you send
Are flattering but true.

Leroy and Lois happily celebrating over 50 years of marriage.

For Better Or For Worse

Your marriage is either going to get better, or it is going to get worse. The direction it takes could depend on you.

Proverbs 14:1 says,
"A wise woman builds her house, while a foolish woman tears hers down by her own efforts."

The foolish woman doesn't decide, "I'm going to tear my house down." What happens is, the house falls down, and she sits there wondering what happened. This is the time for her to evaluate what did happen. Did her marriage fall apart because of things she did or things she didn't do? Had she been wise in her actions and her reactions? The Bible gives us guidelines for being a wise woman.

But, in the middle of a storm is no time to teach someone navigation. My husband and I do quite a bit of traveling by private plane. I felt the need to learn to land the plane in case something happened, and he was unable to land it. So I took a course that taught me the bare essentials: how to find an airport; how to use the radio; and how to land the plane. It is called a pinch-hitter course. If we have a crisis, and it is up to me to land the plane, I have an idea of what to do and how to go about doing it. But during the crisis would be no time for me to begin learning what I would be doing to get that plane on the ground safely.

In marriage we also need to prepare for the crisis before it happens. I hope I will never have to land the plane, but I'm prepared in case I do. Many people think of Biblical principles as something to be used in an emergency. Some consider courses on marriage as pinch-hitter courses to be used in time of crisis. There are others who take all the ground training without ever actually putting it into practice.

I have one friend who has been in a Bible class for years. Her Bible is so marked up. She has a yellow marker that she has used to underline. You can tell by looking at her Bible how much she has studied it. She has had plenty of ground training.

But her marriage reminds me of my tennis game. After thirty years, I decided to take up tennis again. I started taking lessons and learned how to hold my racquet; to stand with my knees slightly bent; to keep my eye on the ball; and so forth. I developed a fairly good forehand and an acceptable backhand. As long as the ball does what I expect, I do fairly well. But the unexpected is what causes me problems. I start swinging wildly and showing no evidence of ever having had even one lesson. At other times, I even look like a tennis player. That is the way it is with my friend. She holds up fairly well when things are just right and even gives instructions to others. You see, she knows the rules of this game called life, but, like me and my tennis game, she needs to practice them.

Biblical principles are given to us, so that we can have the greatest life possible—an abundant life. But we not only need to know the rules, we need to apply them in our everyday life. Another lady I attempted to play tennis with was awful. She didn't know how to stand, how to approach the ball or how to hit. After each shot that she missed, she excused herself with, "I'm really out of practice." The truth of the matter was that she never knew how to play the game in the first place. I knew enough about the game that I could have taught her many things she needed to know, even though I had not had much practical application. But she wasn't teachable. I couldn't teach her anything because she would not admit that she had a need.

The main points of this illustration are:

We need to study God's Word (learn the rules).
We need to apply these rules daily (practice).
We need to be teachable (admit our need and be willing to learn).

Each one of us would like to have a 100% marriage. The problem is: our idea of a 100% marriage may be 20%, our part—80%, his part. That does not add up to 100%, if his idea is 20%, his part, and

80%, your part. If you are willing to go 20%, and he is willing to go 20%, you have a 40% marriage. A 40% marriage can get pretty stormy at times. It should be wife 100% — husband, 100%. Unfortunately, there is often quite a bit of difference between what should be and what is.

HOUSEWORK ISN'T DULL (IF YOU DON'T DO MUCH OF IT)

When I first married, I was not a very good housekeeper. I just plain and simply did not know how. At home we usually had someone around to help with the chores. What that means is, they did it. I had three sisters, and our aim was to do as little as possible, hoping someone would come along and do it for us. Fortunately for Daddy and for us, we also had a cook most of the time. Mama had many wonderful qualities that offset her inability to cook rice that was not all stuck together. One spoonful could bring the entire content up in the air. We always teased her by saying, if we were looking for a place to eat and saw a sign that said "PIES LIKE YOUR MOTHER BAKES," we would go on to the next place. They really weren't that bad, but we did enjoy teasing her.

One day, not long after I was married, my husband came in, looked around, and said, "This apartment is a mess."

You know, he was right; it was a mess. I said, "It sure is, and it's just driving me crazy."

He had made a true statement, and I agreed with him. The fact that I agreed with him didn't make me right, or it didn't make the apartment cleaner, but it did somehow close the conversation. There just wasn't much else to say. He knew it was a mess; I knew it was a mess. The fact was established. But it was also a fact that it was my responsibility to do something about it.

He had taken himself a wife. She was supposed to do "wifey" things. The problem was, I didn't want to do those "wifey" things. I got married so I could quit working. You see, the real problem was, I did not want to assume my responsibility. I was created to be a helper to my husband, and I wasn't holding up my end of the bargain.

I'm sure he wondered many times, "What's a nice boy like me doing in a situation like this?" But I was not concerned with how he felt; I was too busy wondering how I was going to get the apartment cleaned without doing it. One day, he did clean it, to show me how. I told him I was a slow learner. Would he show me again? But he wasn't too taken with that idea.

About now, you are probably saying, "Why was it your responsibility to clean the apartment? Why shouldn't he help?" That was my thinking exactly. "What's a nice girl like me doing in a situation like this?"

He was expecting more of me than I was willing to give. What was I going to do? "I know, I'll go back home." My common sense told me I wouldn't be very welcome if I gave the reason that he expected me to do housework, and I didn't want to do it. I could just hear Mama saying, "But, Lois, that's your responsibility, to keep the house clean." I knew how she felt, even though I didn't exactly know where she had gotten that dumb idea. I also knew that, even though she had someone to do the housework and the cooking most of her married life, it was still her responsibility to see that it was done, and done properly.

After I figured this out, I knew how to solve my problem. I would get a maid. How I "conned" him into letting me have someone to clean a one-room efficiency apartment, I do not remember, but I did.

I thought, "This is great; my problem is solved!" But, even though he had not stopped me from getting a maid, he let me know that he did not like my attitude about cleaning that apartment. I didn't say anything, but I didn't like his attitude about my attitude. I thought that, if I could just get him to change his attitude about my attitude, then everything would be fine. I knew you could catch more flies with honey than with vinegar, so I thought I would try that. I didn't take into consideration that he was smarter than the fly. He knew the honey was not for his benefit; the fly didn't. So that little scheme didn't work out too well. It doesn't take a very smart person to see that, at this point, my marriage was definitely not getting any better. It wasn't too long after this that I started building my "wall."

The Wall

What if you suddenly realized you had built a wall between you and your spouse, or your child, or a neighbor, or a friend? Let me tell you about an experience I had. I built such a wall.

Now you may think reading about a wall will not be very interesting, but it really is. What made this wall so special was that the bricks were transparent.

Our friends and neighbors did not know we were building a wall. If my husband and I were working on it and anyone dropped by, we just did not work on it while they were there.

It was a two faced wall. I built one side and he built the other side.

He did not start out to build a wall. I started the wall to get rid of all those bricks I had piled up.

The foundation was all laid with my bad attitude and self-centeredness.

The more I worked on my wall, the more he felt he needed to do something with his pile of bricks that were just in the way. So, he laid his foundation with anger and bitterness.

Each day I would work on my wall, one day a row of depression, then another one of discontent. I put up two whole rows of anger mixed in with self-pity.

The day I put in a row of self-righteousness, I felt rather peaceful and happy while working on that row.

But I kept right on working until I had another row of discontent and then one of misery.

By the end of the day I was so tired and out of sorts,

I did not feel like fixing supper. My husband refused to take me out to eat so I had to cook and clean up the mess.

Would you believe that after supper I put in another row of self-pity?

It took me a long time, but I finally finished my side of the wall. I built it as high as I could reach, and that was by using the kitchen stool to stand on.

Even after putting in so many hours on my wall, I wasn't happy with it. I did not know what my husband was going to do with his wall, but I decided to tear my side down.

That is exactly what I did, piece by piece, until it was down to the foundation. I just covered up the foundation and decided to take care of it later.

You know what? The funniest thing happened. Well, I think it's funny. His side of the wall was leaning on my side of the wall. When I took my side down, his side fell down. He was really surprised. I thought he might be mad, but he wasn't. He laughed! In fact, we both laughed.

Don't you think it's funny that my wall was holding up his wall? You know something else? I'll bet if he had torn his side down first, my side would have fallen down. Now, you may not think that's funny, but I do.

<u>For He Himself is our peace, who has made the two one and has destroyed the barrier, the dividing wall of hostility.</u> Ephesians 2:14 (NAS)

Not having that wall between us was great, while it lasted, however, leaving the foundation was a big mistake. We should have gotten rid of it instead of covering it up.

With the foundation still in tact, it was easy for us

to build our wall again, and that was exactly what we did. For years we built walls, then tore them down.

It always begins with the foundation. My self-centeredness, along with a bad attitude gave my wall a solid foundation which made it very easy for me to build my side again. He needed to deal with his anger and bitterness.

But how? Just recognizing the problem area is only the beginning. The change begins when some action is taken.

<u>"If we confess our sins, He is faithful and righteous to forgive us our sins and to cleanse us from all unrighteousness."</u> I John 1:9 (NAS)

Walls can also be built between friends, neighbors, business associates, and other family members. The principles of getting rid of them are the same.

The first step is to recognize there is a problem and be willing to take our share of the responsibility. Confession is more than just admitting our wrong doing but to be willing to change directions.

PHASE 1

"But, I Don't Want to be Submissive"

It has become a very popular subject, this business of submitting to your husbands. The courses on marriage really zeroed in on it. And, usually, when the word submission is mentioned in a group of women, you have the same reaction as a group of porcupines about to be attacked by some enemy. I can understand that. It sort of affected me the same way. There is so much information on this subject floating around; some of it good factual information, while some of it is not too realistic or factual. I had gotten just a bit tired of hearing about it.

The impression I got from most of the speakers is that submission is something that God wants you to do (which is true). So just make up your mind, and do it (which is impossible). You don't throw someone out of a boat into deep water without first giving them some instructions in the basics of swimming. Neither do you push someone into the business of submission without giving them some instructions in the basics of the Christian life.

It is not enough for the speaker to understand about the Christian life. That doesn't help any more than the person in the boat knowing how to swim. The one in the water may drown while you are shouting what they are doing wrong. Ephesians 5:21 and Colossians 3:18-21 are the favorite passages used on this subject. Rightly so, since they plainly state the principle. The part that stuck in my mind was, "Wives, submit yourselves unto your own husbands,..." That was what was always emphasized.

It was all very convincing; the Bible said do it, the teacher said do it; former members of the class told glowing reports of how successful it was in their marriage. I believed that was what I should be doing, and still believe it.

I only had one problem with all of this. You see, no matter how much they talked, it didn't change the fact that I just didn't want to do it. Here was a real "do it yourself" project, and I didn't want to do it.

It did cause me enough concern to start looking into the subject. Why, as far as I was concerned, they had skimmed over the most important part. The part that can make it successful. Submit in the same way you submit to the Lord. Here was the key. It wouldn't do any good to concern myself with my relationship to my husband until I had taken care of my relationship with the Lord. Obedience to God is what brings about submission. This was the area I needed to work on.

So far, we have established the need to:
Be teachable (admit our need).
Study God's Word (learn the rules).

Apply these rules (practice).
Be obedient.

And the most important one of all is to be obedient. You may be thinking, "Well, now, that is a big order. I don't know all of these rules yet. How can I obey rules I don't even know?" You begin by being obedient to the rules you do know.

When our children were small, they didn't understand all of the traffic laws. I did not try to teach them all they would need to know to pass the driver's license test. But I did teach them that when the traffic light was green, they could cross the street, but when it was red, they were not supposed to cross. This was something they could understand, and I expected them to obey that traffic law. It was for their benefit that they understood and obeyed this law. As they became more mature, I gradually taught them other laws. The more willing they were to learn, the more I was able to teach them.

God's laws were not given for God's benefit but for our own benefit. So that we can have the greatest life possible.

We begin by being obedient to the laws of God that we do know and understand. As we become more mature, and as we are willing, we can begin learning more of God's laws. The more willing we are to learn, the faster we will learn.

Many times, we are afraid God might require the impossible of us or take away our fun in life. You have no reason to be afraid of a God that has a perfect love for you. He is not out to make you miserable. He is only waiting to give you an abundant life.
In the fourth chapter of I John, it says,

"We need have no fear of someone who loves us perfectly; his perfect love for us eliminates all dread of what he might do to us. If we are afraid, it is for fear of what he might do to us, and shows that we are not fully convinced that he really loves us. So you see, our love for him comes as a result of his loving us first".

As I turned over areas of my life to God, and as He gradually began changing me, He became more real to me. I began getting to know Him better. I began to trust Him with other areas of my life. I became less afraid of what He might do with my life. I did not want to be religious (I still don't want to be religious). And I did not want to lose my identity. But the one area of my life that I hung onto for dear life was my happy spirit – I was born with a happy spirit, and I didn't want to give up my happy spirit. I would say, "Lord, do anything you want to with my life, but don't take away my happy spirit."

It was only a few months ago that I finally said, "O.K., Lord – I release my happy spirit to you; whatever you do with me I will accept, because I know you love me and what you have in mind for me is better than what I have in mind for myself." Only when I was willing to release this to God, did I realize that God has given me my happy spirit, and that He would not take it from me unless He could use me better without it. So far, nothing drastic has taken place; he hasn't taken away my happy spirit or my sense of humor. God has a happy Spirit, because what God's Spirit produces in us is love – joy –peace – patience – kindness — goodness – faithfulness – gentleness – and self-control. A person with all those qualities will truly have a happy spirit.

Let's pray – you talk to God in your own way. That's really all that prayer is – talking to God. Tell Him what your needs are. If you need Him to come into your life, then ask Him to come in. You can say, "Lord Jesus, I want you to come into my life – to forgive my sins – and become my Lord and Master and to make me the kind of person you want me to be."

Maybe you need to pray a prayer like the one the young minister's wife prayed; "Father, you see all of these things in my life that are displeasing to you. I agree they are sin; they are not mistakes – they are sins. I ask you to forgive me, and I thank you that you have, because you said you would. Take control of my life and live it through me."

Whatever your need – just talk to God about it.

Dear Heavenly Father -
        I thank you for the being my Heavenly Father.
        I thank you for loving me -for being so patient with me.

I thank you for what you have done in my life so far.
I thank you for what you are going to continue to do in my life.
Getting to know you better is exciting.
Make me more and more like you.

I pray this in the Name of Jesus Christ. Amen.

PHASE TWO

THE PLACE OF TOTAL COMMITMENT

When I arrived at "The Place of Total Commitment", I couldn't find any place to park my Lincoln Continental. I had driven over in it, because I felt it would be a good thing for the other people there to see that I had not come out of desperation; that I wasn't in any financial bind; that I came because I really wanted to. But there was not a place to park, even for a moment. It was very crowded in front of this place – so many people milling around.

Since there wasn't any place to park, I took the car home and walked over. It was a much shorter distance than I thought. It seems I had been very close to this place for a long time without realizing it. I made my way through the crowd to the entrance. There, I was told to leave my jewelry and the keys to my car. Although I had often said jewelry didn't mean anything to me, I didn't really want to give it up. My wedding band was evidence of my commitment to my husband, and I would like to keep the earrings, because I had those holes in my ears; and, really, the diamonds weren't that big. They assured me they would be kept in a safe place and would be returned on demand, or given back to me if, in any way, I could use them "for the glory of God." So, I did as they asked.

It had taken me a long time to decide to come to

this "Place of Total Commitment." I was ready – so very ready – to do "great things for God" and was very anxious to get on with it.

I looked back at the crowd – they had all come to the threshold of this place but were not able to make up their minds to come in.

"Listen, God, if you are wondering what to do with me, I think I could be a big help just working with these people. You know, I meet people well and can talk to almost anyone. Of course, I would need my jewelry and my car if you would provide me with a place to park. I know I could convince lots of these people to come on in."

Well, it was just a thought, but God didn't indicate in any way that this was what He had for me to do, so I just went on in.

It was a very large room...like the old train stations. There were several groups of people sitting around. There were many people milling around besides the ones that had joined the various groups.

One group was singing. I walked over to hear what they were singing – "Let's just praise the Lord, praise the Lord. Let's just lift our voices to heaven and praise the Lord."

It was very pretty, but just sitting around praising the Lord wasn't my idea of what I wanted to do. I can't sing very well anyway. That wasn't what I was looking for.

The next group were all down on their knees. I couldn't hear what they were saying, but I knew they were praying. I had done an awful lot of that – that's how I had gotten to this place. I was impressed with seeing such a large group down on their knees, praying, but I didn't stop there. That wasn't what I was looking for.

The next group was a Bible Study group. Everyone had an open Bible in their laps and were in deep concentration and meditation. I would have like to join that group, but I didn't have time to stop. That wasn't what I was looking for.

Then, I saw what I had been looking for – Service Entrance. I had come there to serve. I dashed out the entrance, passed several people that were coming back in.

Just ahead of me was a boarding platform. On one side were quite a few red telephones with a sign over them "HOT LINE TO HEAVEN." On the other side were benches and some rather large bookracks – could hold 50-60 books, maybe more. There was a sign that read "PLEASE BE SEATED AND WAIT FOR YOUR NAME TO BE CALLED." I decided to get a book and read while I waited. Some books had hardly been touched; they looked almost brand-new, but others were worn. You could tell which were the favorites. I could understand because I had read parts of all of the new-looking ones but didn't have much interest in them. I decided to read the one on the very bottom that must have been a real favorite. This book of Revelation was barely readable. It has been so misused by so many that I just put it back. I read a little from the book of John but couldn't seem to get into it. I tried the book of James, but I couldn't seem to get my mind on any of them I was so anxious to get moving that I just wasn't interested in reading.

I thought maybe I would walk back inside, just to see what was going on in there. I didn't want to join any of the groups because I was afraid I might not hear them call my name. I found out later that they had a P.A. system, and I could have joined a group and still heard my name when it was called. I also learned that many of these people had been in the Bible Study group for a long time before they had been called.

Instead of going inside I thought I would use the phone. I picked it up and got a signal that my call had gone through.

"Lord, I guess you don't know how much I want to do great things for you. (Excuse me Lord. Since you know everything about me, you do know.) But I just wanted to talk to you about it. Lord, I'm willing for you to fly me to any spot to serve you, no matter how far; I've always loved to travel, you know."

"Trust me" was the reply.

It was a long time before my name was called. I couldn't seem to settle down. I would read a little and then walk around, and then sit and not do anything. It seemed that most of the people that were waiting to be called were doing the same thing. I don't think I have ever seen a more impatient group.

There were no planes in, when they called my name. But, as I walked up to the boarding platform, I was handed the envelope containing my jewelry and my car keys. Then, a taxi pulled up. This wasn't what I had expected and started to try to get back to the phone. But I had waited so long already that I just got in, and we pulled out of the station.

"Pardon me. Please excuse me! Could I get through, please?" I was back at "The Place of Total Commitment." This time, I knew where to go and rushed through the Service Entrance and to the phones. "Lord," I shouted, "They made a mistake – they took me back to my house." Just between you and me (I didn't say this to the Lord), but it was a good thing I did go by – the maid had not come, and there were some things I needed to do. But I hurried and did them, so I could rush back.

Do you know, I got the same answer I had gotten before – "Trust me." I said to the person on the next phone, "Do you think maybe that's a recording and not really a Hot Line to Heaven?" I thought I'd try once more. "Listen, God."

A voice came on, saying, "You have been temporarily disconnected." I said, "Oh, darn!" I tried several more times but couldn't seem to get through.

That was when I learned about the P.A. system in the other room. So I joined the Bible Study group while I waited. They were studying Philippians. That was one of the books that had been worn and used-looking on the bookrack. The second chapter was where they were when I joined them. I had missed the first one. I was reminded that God is at work in me but not doing what I want, but what He wants. I guess I will just have to trust Him, no matter what He has willed for me to do. Maybe I'm needed at home. I also was reminded to look out for need and interest of others – not just my own interest. Maybe I should go back home and do more Bible Study.

On the way, I passed the prayer group, I knelt down to talk to God. I realized I didn't have to use the red phone. "Lord, you may not need me, but I sure need you. No matter what you have for me to do will be fine. I do trust you. If you want me, I'll be at home. Just give me a call"

Dear Janie,

I'm excited and happy about your commitment to God's will for your life. I had said before, it would be so great if you could get your priorities in order – that, if God could have your complete attention, I knew He could use you in a mighty way.

Since I made this commitment, several years ago, I have been in the process of learning exactly what God's plan is for my life.

I can tell you one thing. It isn't what I thought it would be. I have many abilities (I feel) that God is not using. So I've almost decided to give up on many areas of my life and wait. You see, that's one step toward total commitment. Wait...

"Abiding in the vine," the Bible calls it...

For so many years, I prayed for God to use me. I had common sense. I could clearly see the problems of others and knew what the solution was for them. But, somehow, I couldn't get my "Doing Great Things for God" project off the ground. I couldn't understand it. Here I was, willing – anxious – available. You know what I mean: Why wasn't God using me more? I knew He was using me in the lives of some, but why wasn't He using me in the lives of others? I had so much more capability that responsibility (I thought). I can honestly say that my motives were right, a far as I can remember, (As right as motives can be when we are doing what we are doing in our strength.)

More and more, I'm realizing that God's plan for my life is to accept the God-given responsibility that I have now; being the wife of a very active husband. That is another thing I'm learning gradually.

WAIT – ACCEPT.

I do have time for <u>Bible Study,</u> time to <u>pray</u>, time to minister on a one-to-one basis. Even though I am not in a leadership position, many times God has given me the opportunity to minister to people in leadership situations.

When I try and share how I'm serving the Lord, what great and might things I am doing for God, I don't seem to be doing any great and mighty things. But I can <u>pray.</u> I can <u>study the Bible.</u>

WAIT – ACCEPT – PRAY – BIBLE STUDY.

I can minister on a one-to-one basis if I'm available to God. God does use me in the lives of individuals if I'm <u>available.</u>

<u>WAIT–ACCEPT–PRAY–BIBLE STUDY–BE AVAILABLE</u>

I'm learning lots of things: God doesn't need me; I need Him. God doesn't want me running His business; He wants to run mine. I have no capabilities, only gifts from God to be used by God when it suits His purpose.

I can just sit back and let God do His work in me and through me. I'm only one little faucet. I don't need to turn myself on. But it is so very exciting when God allows some of His living water to flow through my spigot.

At this point in my life, I'm more teachable than I've ever been. It really is a new beginning for me.

Do let's keep in touch.

Love,
Lois

PHASE THREE

"LORD, TEACH ME MY ROLE AS A WIFE.

In the second chapter of Genesis, it tells us that God created a companion for Adam, so he wouldn't have to be alone. She was created to be a helper suited to Adam's needs.

There was a time when I thought that being a helper meant – help him pick out a secretary – help him run his business, and so forth. I was quick to learn that wasn't acceptable to my husband and slow to learn that wasn't acceptable to God.

Eve's duties were not the same as mine. They didn't have any clothes, so she didn't have to bother about doing the laundry – no house, so no housecleaning – no car, no car pool – no bills! Wow! Sounds like paradise.

Since each husband has different needs, each wife has a different role. That is why the Bible doesn't give a job description for a wife. Each wife must write her own job description.

At the present time, I am a housewife without a house, married to a businessman without a business. Even so, he is very active, a real "ball of fire." And, as you might have gathered, I'm pretty much a "ball of fire," myself. But a "ball of fire" doesn't need another "ball of fire". A "ball of fire" needs someone standing there with a bucket of water, figuratively speaking.

Literally speaking, there are times when he needs me to stop talking and just listen. If he isn't doing much talking, it may be he is having a problem getting a word in edgewise. He knows more about almost everything than I do, but I do most of the talking.

"LORD, TEACH ME TO BE A GOOD LISTENER."

Proverbs 21:23 (LB) says,
"Keep your mouth closed and you'll stay out of trouble."

I thought that sound a little flippant, but the King James Version says, "Whosoever keepeth his mouth and his tongue keepeth his soul from trouble."

I need practice being a good listener. A good listener is always in demand. Just listening enables you to be tuned into the thoughts and interests of the other person.

Proverbs 19:20 (RSV)
"Listen to advice and accept instruction that you may gain wisdom for the future."

In the first chapter of James, it says we should be quick to hear and slow to speak.

Since each person has a different need, I would like to just toss out some practical suggestions. Maybe you will recognize a need in your life and be able to deal with your own particular need.

If he does talk to you, show a genuine interest in what he has to say. **Be sincere.** Don't try and fake it – it won't work! In a relationship as intimate as marriage, it does not take long for the veneer to wear thin, and a lack of genuineness to show through.

Be creative in how you handle situations. Sometimes the way we approach a problem doesn't take much creativity. When he is walking out the door on his way to work, is not time to have a family conference about the repairs that are needed around the house or anything else. When he comes home and is worn out, don't meet him at the door with all the problems of the day.

When your husband comes home, **be sensitive** to his moods. Take the pressure off him when he's under stress. Do you know when he's under stress? By the way he slams the car door – or the way he speaks – or the way he doesn't speak. If you work at it, you will learn. You can smooth the way by your quiet spirit.

Proverbs 15:4 (LB)
"Gentle words cause life and health; griping brings discouragement."

Show respect for your husband. Respect him as an individual. Never make fun of him – even in fun. Women who ridicule and belittle their husbands only defeat themselves.

"LORD, TEACH ME TO BE SENSITIVE TO HIS NEEDS"

When a man and woman marry and establish a home, the man is the head of this home He should be like the RIM of a wheel – to be a protective cushion between the family and the world, taking the jolts and the hardships.

I realize many men are not fulfilling their role. But we are not trying to straighten the men out. This is a Bible Study designed for women, so that you can learn how to better fulfill your role as a wife, mother, and a homemaker.

The woman should be like the HUB of the wheel. Everything in the home revolves around her. As the hub goes, so goes the wheel. If the hub is off-center, the whole wheel is thrown off-balance. What does that do to the atmosphere of the home? It throws the whole household in a turmoil. It is very unnerving to a man to always be wondering what mood his wife will be in when he comes home. He would like to come home to a happy well-adjusted situation. But, more often than not, he finds his household in a turmoil.

We can be a magnet that draws him from all roads home to us, or we can be a repellent that drives him away from us. We can have the kind of home that is a pleasure to come to or the kind of home that makes him dread coming home.

Have you ever thought, "If I could just get my husband to change, then everything would be fine, and we could be happy." The best reason I can think of for not trying to change him is – you're not going to change him. God can change him, but you can't. Continually trying to change him can cause problems in your marriage. It may cause him to rebel. Our tendency is to take things into our own hands instead of trusting God with the situation. Accept your husband as he is. Being accepted and admired by his wife is an important element in a man's life. <u>It is difficult for a man to feel tenderly</u>

toward a woman who is always trying to change him. Do you know of one man who stopped smoking because his wife told him he was killing himself by smoking so much? He may have been doing just that, but her attempt to make him stop was not the solution. He was the one that had to decide. God gave man the freedom of choice. We take away man's freedom by our disapproval, our suggestions, nagging and criticism. Every man wants to live in peace. Every man wants approval. You need to help your husband to learn to accept himself. You can help him do this by loving him and accepting him, faults and all. So much of the time, it is very difficult for husbands to live up to our expectations of them and still fulfill his God-given responsibilities.

What are some of the things that you expect from him? That he tells you often that he loves you? That he remembers your birthday? That he sends you flowers? Any action you demand from your husband doesn't amount to much anyway. A dutiful husband may do and say these things without any actual feelings toward his wife. If you want to win his heart and his love, accept him as he is. Don't keep trying to change him. Remember that God can work in your husband's life without your husband knowing it. God can work in his life without you knowing it, either.

Each person has to look at his own situation and ask God's help. You may not understand the circumstances you are in. You may not understand the love of God either. "What does God's love have to do with the situation I am in, now?" God wants you to trust Him with this situation. "But I do."—"I trust God." "I really believe He is going to change my husband."

You may be praying for the wrong person to change. You may be the one that needs to do some changing. When we see another at fault, then is the time for self-examination. For so many years, I prayed for God to change my husband's mind about me. I prayed, "Lord, help him to accept me – just as I am." I wanted to be the way I wanted to be, but I wanted him to change. God didn't seem to be answering my "earnest" prayer. And I really prayed believing. Finally, I said, "Lord, help me to accept the fact that he doesn't accept me." You know, my whole attitude changed. I had come to the place where I was willing to let God change my attitude about the situation. That was one step in the right direction, even though my motives were not what they should have been.

Are you thinking, "Why do I have to do all the changing?" "Doesn't God expect the same thing from my husband that He expects from me?" God does demand the same thing from your husband that He demands of you. But none of what God demands of you is conditioned on how well your husband meets God's demands of him. Your husband is not hearing this. God is talking to you. It is your responsibility you have to face. Trust God with your situation, no matter whether the problem is large or small.

Many problem situations are caused from our wrong attitude. Women can think up more excuses for being moody, out of sorts and depressed. We can just think ourselves into a bad mood. Many times, the things we think about cause us as much trouble as the things we do. Often-times, the problem did not stem from an action of another person, but from our own reaction. We react by feeling sorry for ourselves (everything is wrong – nobody likes me, etc.) Our critical spirit shows up. We feel mistreated – slighted.

This is the time we should take our spiritual temperature. We should examine our heart before God. How? Ask ourselves, "What's wrong with my <u>attitude?</u>" "Is this bad mood self-inflicted by my own self-centeredness?" "Why am I so moody and depressed?" If we do have a concern, moodiness and depression won't solve anything.

The Bible says:
Let Him have all your worries and cares, for He is always thinking about you and watching everything that concerns you." (I Peter 5:7, LB)

God is watching me. What does He see? A very negative person? When my thoughts become just plain negative, then I'm not the least bit excited about life. If I'm not excited about life, there is something wrong with my relationship with God. Maybe I should try and get in touch with God to find out what's wrong.

Operator

Operator, I would like to put in a call to Heaven, station to station."

"I'm sorry Ma'am, they do not accept station to station calls. What is the party's name that you wish to call?"

"Could you just put in a call to God?"

"Unless you have a number, I will not be able to help you. If you dial 411, information may be able to give you the number." "Information, I am trying to get in touch with God. Could you give me a number where I could reach Him?"

"Is that listed under just G - O - D, no initials?

"I guess so."

"I'm sorry, but I do not have a listing like that."

"Would you look for a number for Jesus Christ?"

"Ma'am, I do have a listing for that party but I am not allowed to give out that information."

"Operator, I really do need to talk to Him. Isn't there anyway I can get the number?"

"You might try your minister. He may be able to help you get in touch with the party. I'm sorry, I cannot help you."

"Listen Operator, try Holy Spirit. I am sure you have a listing for Him."

"There are several listings for that party. If you will give me the first three digits of the number you are calling from, I will give you the number nearest you."

"I'm calling from the 426 exchange."

"I do have a 426 number, 426-1111. You may dial direct."

"Operator, that is the number I am calling from. You mean He lives here?"

"I do not know Ma'am, that is the number I have listed. Don't you know if He lives there?"

"No, I really did not know that He was around. Thank you, Operator. I'll try to contact Him here."

"Holy Spirit, I need to talk to you. It sure is hard to talk to someone you can't see. Could You just let me know if you are here? Don't touch me because that would really scare me."

"I know that Jesus said He would have to go away but He would send His Spirit to live in me, and that His Spirit would show me when I am wrong, then show me the right way. I know my attitude is most of the problem, but I haven't been very successful at changing it myself. I definitely need help with that. I also read that You are supposed to create in me many things that I don't see any evidence of, like self-control, gentleness, goodness, as well as peace and joy.

"Are You really living in me?"

"You are not in the flesh but in the Spirit, if indeed the Spirit of God dwells in you. Now if anyone does not have the Spirit of Christ in him, he is not His."

Romans 8:9 (NKJ)

Neglected

I'm so sore I can hardly move,
　　I know it's only a muscle
The yardman was here yesterday
　　　and the two of us did hustle.
When my head starts hurting
　　and feels of pain,
Could it just be I've used
　　my neglected brain?

Baby

She is having a baby
Would be filled with glee
Except for the fact
Babies come C. O. D.

It's Over

I held the blanket
    It moved
    I touched
    It cried
Pink and soft
    She was real
    She was mine

No place to go
No one to care
    I Care
    He said to me
    You are Mine

I held the blanket
    It moved
    She was real
    She was mine
Little one, don't cry
    He is here
    He cares

Chapter Four

A Growing Commitment

Chapter Four

(The Place of Total Commitment) Cont'd

This was written several years ago in response to a letter I received from a friend. She said, "I know that you have been praying for me and I just wanted you to know that I have finally come to the place of total commitment." I felt that I knew what it meant to be totally committed but that she didn't. And it was true that she didn't, but neither did I.

The Place of Total Commitment is my story also and has ministered to me through the years. "Trust Me" has come through loud and clear. Can I trust God in any situation? When I stop trusting Him am I temporarily disconnected? Have you also come to the place of total commitment but at times find yourself temporarily disconnected?

My husband and I spent almost 6 months in Israel. We rented an apartment in Bethlehem and it certainly was not what I had been accustomed to. The house was stone and held the cold in winter and summer. Summer was all right but it was winter when we moved in. One of the main problems was the antiquated plumbing. The basin in the bathroom leaked all over the floor and every time the toilet flushed, it sounded like Niagara Falls, complete with spray. Because the bowl was cracked, water ran out all over our feet. I also stood in a puddle of cold water when I stood at the sink washing dishes. I was not very happy with the whole situation. The weather was cold, the apartment was cold, and I was cold.

Trying to set up a household in a foreign country was quite a job. Housework had never been a favorite pastime of mine and dish washing was the least of all. To have to do it standing in a puddle of cold water was just too much. It had been years since I had come to the place of saying, "God, I want to be what You want me to be." Even if it meant just being a wife of this very busy husband that He had given me. As some of you might know, my husband is a real ball of fire. And I am pretty much a ball of fire myself. So one thing that I had to learn was, a ball of fire does not need another ball of fire. What a ball of fire needs is someone standing there with a bucket of water. So I was really surprised at myself for getting so upset about a few dishes that needed washing and some water on the floor.

If you had only known me in the early years of our marriage, it would be very evident that I had indeed come a long way from where I started. When I first married, I thought, "This nice young man is going to work everyday, and I can stay home and do what I want to do." He had a different idea. He thought that while he was out working, I would be at home doing those things wives do; cooking, cleaning, washing everything (clothes, dishes, windows, etc.). I was much more interested in getting a suntan than in cleaning house.

Truthfully, I did not know much about keeping a house clean. I was raised in the south and we usually had someone around to help with the chores. Mama didn't know much about it either. Her idea was that house cleaning should be done with as much ease as possible and not to get too uptight about it. This attitude carried over into the kitchen as well. She had many wonderful qualities that offset her inability to cook rice that was not all stuck together. One dip into the bowl could bring the entire content up in the air.

That happened almost 40 years ago. I thought that problem had been solved years ago. But here I was in Bethlehem, standing at the sink in a puddle of cold water, washing dishes with a bad attitude. I definitely was disconnected. By this time in my life I had learned that the Bible had answers for all of our problems and I knew that my attitude was what was causing me to lose my peace. I looked up attitude in Strong's concordance and do you know what? It wasn't even listed. I decided that the Bible must call it something else. So I looked it up in the dictionary to see what it had to say.

Webster says: Attitude, a manner of feeling or thinking that shows ones disposition, opinion, etc.

The Bible says, "As she thinkest in her heart, so is she."

It really says 'he" but I know it means "me" so I put "she." If I'm thinking that I'm not interested in trusting God with the responsibility that He has given me, then I won't be, and it will become a mountainous task, almost too big to climb over. What am I really trying to say? Not anything that you do not already know, but it helps sometimes to be reminded of it.

In Galatians Paul tells us that the fruit of the Spirit of God is love, peace, joy, patience, kindness, goodness, faithfulness.

If I am not experiencing the peace of God, then I am

disconnected. How temporarily it is, is up to me. What is it that has caused me to lose contact with the Spirit of God? A little three letter word— SIN.

Is it a sin to not like to wash dishes? If it causes me to lose my peace, then it sure is. My circumstances do not create my attitude, they just reveal my spirit.

I took my neighbor to a Bible study. She was not a Christian at this time. The teacher said that we all had sinned and we need to confess our sins. My neighbor was a good person and she did not like the idea at all that the teacher said she was a sinner. In fact, she was very offended at the teacher and at me for taking her to the Bible class. I tried to tell her that we were all sinners, but she didn't buy that either. I spent a lot of time praying for her and for guidance in how I could get her straightened out about this.

It was several weeks before I realized that it was not my job to convince her that she was a sinner. Jesus said that when the Holy Spirit comes, He will convict men of their sin. I decided what she needed was to get in touch with the Spirit of God through reading the Word. But I did not run right over with a Bible at this time. I was just a friend to her. She was not well and I tried to help anyway that I could and never mentioned again about us being sinners. We did become friends and I had the opportunity to offer her a Living Bible after she had done something very nice for me. Along with it I gave her the Daily Walk which is a Bible Study that takes you through the Bible in one year.

Several months went by and one day she said, "I found out I'm a sinner."

I said, "Really, how did you find that out?"

"From reading the Bible. It really isn't all that bad, is it?"

I thought that was a funny remark. But it really isn't when you know what to do about it. Just knowing about sin is not the answer, it is not doing it that gets results.

I definitely was not trusting God with the damp leaky apartment. When I finally realized this, I committed the whole situation to my Heavenly Father. I admitted it was sin and I asked forgiveness. Even though I had all of this information, it wasn't until I acted on it that I found my peace. And I wasn't disconnected anymore. It was a simple repair job after all. The next day the plumber came and fixed all of the leaks. And I learned that God can use whatever comes into our lives for good if we let Him—even a cold damp apartment.

Noah and Me

God did promise Noah and his family that He would never destroy the earth again by a flood. But in the 9th chapter, He also made some other promises, verses 1, 2, 3 and 6. What were these promises?

1.the continuation of the human race (v 1)

2. that birds and beast would fear humans (v 2)

3. the repeated promise that humans will have do minion over land and sea(v 2)

4. the amazing promise, "I give you everything" (v 3)

5. the promise on which human government is based, the assurance that human beings will be able to live together in a society(v 6)

God had told Adam and Eve to be fruitful and multiply, and fill the earth.

In this chapter He is telling Noah and his family the same thing.

In the 15th verse God tells Noah what? That He will never bring another flood to destroy the whole earth?

What did Noah do in the 20th verse?

It is obvious that Noah trusted God's word because he began planting and farming the land.

Scattered throughout the Bible are 3000 promises to us from God.

Look up these verses

Ps 50:15 - Matt. 7:7 - Rom. 10:13 - Phil. 4:19 - John 11-25 -Rom. 8-28.

God is never loose with His promises but we are, aren't we? Has your child ever said, "I wont ever do that again, I promise," and then goes out and does it again.

Do any of you ever lose your temper and promise yourself, "never again?"

The history of Noah is a beautiful presentation of trusting God. God showed himself faithful. Can you just imagine Noah building a big boat on dry land and no water anywhere around?

So much for Noah. Let's talk about us.

Does anyone here disagree with the fact that we can trust God and His Word?

But, do you trust Him?

Do you think that trusting means, trusting God to work things out like we want them. If they don't work out to our satisfaction we stop trusting and start complaining. In my opinion, there is a direct connection between total commitment and trusting.

Commitment is a choice. Have you read "<u>Happiness is a Choice</u>"? Well, so is commitment.

Many years ago I heard a woman speak at a conference at the Fountainblue Hotel in Miami Beach. She challenged us to let God be God in every area of our life. "Are you willing to turn complete control of your life over to God?"

Do you know what? I wasn't willing. I was afraid that if I said that, God would take all the fun out of my life. I knew that I should do just that, but I wasn't willing.

Then she said, "If you are not willing, are you willing to be made willing?"

Oh yes, I said to myself. I am willing to be made willing.

So that was my prayer and do you know what? I found out that I was willing to let God take charge. I wasn't very mature, but I was willing to do whatever God had for me to do.

The rainbow is not just pretty to see
It's a reminder of God's promise to me

Swim

I love to swim, I really do
But what I most regret
There is absolutely no other way
Except to get all wet.

Operator Two Or Feed My Sheep

"Hello, may I please speak to the Master? O. K., I'll wait."

"Master, I'm the shepherd down here with Your sheep. I saw this farm house had a telephone and decided to call about a problem I think You should know about."

"What did You say? Have many new sheep been arriving?

"Yes Sir, quite a few arrive each day. In fact, these new sheep are what I'm calling about.

"No, they are not sick. At least I don't think they are. As soon as they arrive, we all run down to the pond and get a refreshing drink of cool water. I pat each one on the head, tell them how glad we are to have them join our flock, and try to make them feel welcome. I sing and play the harp and encourage them to join in. I even invited the shepherd band to come over and play for them."

"Some of the new sheep enjoy being entertained and stay with the group. But many of them lag behind, with little interest in what we are doing."

"Do You have any suggestions?"

"Am I feeding them? Yes Sir, once a day. Every morning first thing, I feed all of them."

"Oh, You say spend more time feeding them than trying to entertain. How much more food should I give them?"

"All they want! If I were to do that, it would mean feeding them all day. Those new ones are so hungry when they first arrive. The old ones stopped wanting so much food after they get used to being fed only once a day."

"Am I giving them a balanced diet? Do You think

that may be part of the problem?"

"It may be. I'll stop trying to entertain them and start feeding them more often. It may help if I pay more attention to what kind of food I give them. This might keep some of the old ones from drifting away."

"Thank You, Sir. I appreciate being able to talk to You. I have to get back to the sheep now but will call again real soon to let You know how things are going."

"You say I should get in touch with You at least once a day? Really? Every day? It will be hard to find the time but I will try. Thanks again for Your help today. I guess I should call more often, even when I don't have a problem."

"Master, this is the shepherd again. Am I calling at a bad time?"

"You are glad to hear from me anytime? That is great."

"I just wanted to tell You I changed the sheep's diet and started feeding them more often. I followed the instructions You gave me about what to feed them. You know what? They started growing."

"They really did. I can see a big difference in them, already. I appreciate Your help."

"Thanks. I will be keeping in touch."

So Weary

Weary,
   Need rest
      Too much to do
      Can't rest

Lord, help me
   I cried

I'm weary,
   Need rest
      Too much to do
      Can't rest

He heard my cry
   He answered me

Weary child
   Come to Me
      I will
         Give you rest

"Come to Me, all who are weary and
heavy-laden, and I will give you rest."
                    Matthew 11:28 (NAS)

Aerial view of the Eger family home at Lighthouse Point, Florida, during the late 1970's. In the background on the canal is the 63 foot Motor Yacht used by the Egers' to travel up and down the Intracoastal and teach at various churches studies pertaining to the Lay Institute as well as encouraging ministers from all over the world.

I Was Set Up

At the trial I was not allowed to hear any other testimony. The newspaper account mentioned an informant and some other things that were confusing. After I demanded to see it, the assistant district attorney only allowed me to read the transcript of the trial in his office.

"The detectives watched three masked men enter my house and did not try to stop them!" I shouted. "Why? They knew I was alone. I could have been killed."

I could not believe what I was reading—that two detectives waited outside my house for over an hour after they saw men break in my house.

It had been almost six months since that horrible night. I arrived home about 9 P.M. after visiting my husband in the hospital. It had been a long tiring day, so I retired early.

A loud CRASH woke me up with a start. Instantly, I knew what was happening. Someone was breaking down my bedroom door.

"Surely, this can not be happening to me." I remember checking the dead bolt before going to bed. The only way anyone could get into my bedroom was to break down the door and that was exactly what was happening.

A second CRASH. I saw a foot come through the door and it flew open. I cried out to the Lord, "Oh God, are You going to let me die?" I was on my feet screaming when a man grabbed me. Another man said, "Gag her, she has already made enough noise." "Tie her hands behind her back," another one shouted. Someone pulled a pillow case over my head. How many are there, two, maybe three? The one who had kicked the door down had some sort of gray thing over his head and face. The others were behind me so I did not get a look at them. I was gasping for breath and could not seem to get enough air.

Someone pushed me from the back and I fell face down on the floor with no way to catch myself.

"Oh God, I cannot believe this is happening to me. I'm at the mercy of these men. What am I going to do?"

A Bible verse came to my mind. "In all things give thanks, for this is the will of God."

This certainly did not seem appropriate for my situation. I was scared out of my wits and could hardly breathe. My heart was pounding so hard it was shaking my whole body.

Give thanks? Why? For what? For being tied up with strange men in my bedroom, not knowing what they were going to do to me?

The same verse flashed through my mind again. "In all things give thanks, for this is the will of God."

"Tie her feet together," barked the one who seemed to be giving the orders.

"Thank You, Lord." Many women are raped which must be a horrible degrading experience.

"Where's the stuff?" a very rough talking man said as he leaned over me. "I am going to kill you if you don't tell me where the stuff is."

He grabbed my left hand and noticed my wedding rings. "Give me these," he barked as he tried to pull them off.

"I have to soap my finger to get them off." I could talk even though it was muffled.

"Never mind, I'll just cut them off."

Surely he's not going to cut my finger off. But what else could he mean? I was helpless to do anything but wait.

"Just leave them alone," one of them said. I was so

relieved and thankful when he dropped my hand.

The same verse came to mind again.

"Heavenly Father, I do not understand why this is happening to me but even in this situation I will say, `Thank You'."

Although they had already threatened to kill me several times, I was still alive. That was one thing I could be thankful for.

I'm thankful they have not raped me or cut off my finger.

"O God, thank You for being with me and protecting me in this awful situation. Thank You for my guardian angel who must be protecting and watching over me."

After I finished praying that prayer, an amazing thing happened. Amidst all of the turmoil I began to experience an inner peace.

Peace! at a time like this, unbelievable. I was still scared on the outside, but on the inside I had a calmness that was unexplainable.

"Can I really trust God with this terrible predicament?" I thought. Somehow, I knew that I could.

My situation had not changed but there was a definite change in me. My breathing had leveled off and was not such a struggle.

At first, the men did not speak directly to me. I could hear muffled sounds of talking. I had heard the music box, where I kept my jewelry, play briefly while I was being tied up.

Something cold and pointed touched my neck. I knew it was a knife. "What's he going to do now?" flashed through my mind.

"Where's the stuff? We are going to kill you if you don't tell us where the stuff is."

"What stuff do you mean?" I asked.

"Your diamonds, your gold, your money."

He sounded agitated, as if he had not found any of the jewelry. I knew someone had found our diamonds because they were in the drawer that made the music box play.

"Tell us where the stuff is. We are going to kill you." By now I was able to answer him very calmly.

"The jewelry in that music box is all I have."

"Where is your money?" I told him where to find three $50 bills.

"Where's the rest of your money?" he barked.

"It's in the bank."

For about 45 minutes they rummaged, dumping drawers, asking questions, poking me with that knife and threatening to kill me. I tried to cooperate with them, hoping they would find what they were looking for and leave.

Finally, one of them came back and threatened me again.

"If you try and get loose, we really will kill you."

I thought I heard them run out the front door. It got very quiet. I did manage to free my hands. The gag was very tight, but I pulled it down and took the pillow case off. Their warning came to my mind, so I put the pillow case back on my head and lay down with my hands tucked under me. A motor boat went down the canal.

Maybe they left by boat. "Dear God, please let me know when it is safe to get up."

After awhile I got up, and that is when I noticed the blood. I had been stabbed but was so scared I did not even know it. I held my leg to stop the blood from flowing so freely, hobbled into the bathroom, and after quietly closing the door and locking it, I dialed the operator. When the police arrived, they seemed very glad to find me alive.

"Two of the men have been caught," they said, "and

there might be a third one."

"Are you all right?" one of them asked.

"Only my leg, but it is not bad, I didn't even know it. He said excitedly, "Have the medics come quick and look at her leg. She's been stabbed."

"You seem very calm after such an ordeal."

"I know," I answered, "It just has to be the Lord. I'm not all that brave."

Those nice concerned detectives were the ones who had watched the three masked men enter my house. It is not surprising they were glad to find me alive. I'm sure they had misgivings over their unwise decision after they heard me let loose that blood curdling scream and then silence. It must have been a very long wait for them, not knowing what was happening in the house.

The man who kicked the door down was an informant for the sheriff's department. That was their excuse for not stopping them from breaking into my house. He was the one who took the jewelry. The sheriff's department allowed him to get away.

While the other two were tying me up, he took the diamonds out of the music box and put them in his pocket. His helpers were not aware of this. That is why they were so agitated that they could not find the jewelry they had come for.

After the trial the informant disappeared and so did our most valuable jewelry.

Can I still give thanks in all things? Yes, I can. I can even be thankful that there was an informant because he knew the detectives were out there. He could get away with robbery but not rape or murder.

The loss of jewelry cannot be compared with being raped or losing one's life. God met me at my point of need and gave me the peace I needed to get me through that awful ordeal.

"In all things, give thanks, for this is the will of God."

Chapter Five

A Pathway
to Peace

or

"Rusty Armor"

Chapter Five

The Pathway To Peace or "Rusty Armor"

I had my book of instructions and was gathering up the rest of the armor when I realized my sandals of peace were missing. After looking all over the house and my car, I called Susan to ask if I had left them there.

"I haven't seen them. Why not try your pathway to peace? You may find them there."

I knew that was probably where I had lost them but I definitely did not want to go there. It was such a dark and dreary place with huge bags of garbage almost blocking the pathway and trash scattered all around.

Cleaning up a pile of garbage was not what I had in mind and I considered climbing over it. Since my sandals might be in the middle of it, there was no way for me to know unless I took time to clean up the whole pathway.

The first obstacle I had to deal with was a large bag

of self. Some seeds had fallen out and taken root. Large bushes had sprouted up in the middle of the trash pile. Some were as big as trees. This was obviously going to be quite a job.

One of the main difficulties would be to distinguish between the plants to leave in the path and the ones to take out. Some of the bushes of self-righteousness looked rather nice. But, all of the self-pity ones were ugly and needed to be removed. The self-centeredness bush was so big and ugly, it would definitely have to go.

First, I had to cut down all of those undesirables and get rid of them. Then the roots needed to be dug up or the bushes would just grow back bigger than they were before. Although some of the bushes of self-righteousness seemed attractive at first glance, I noticed they were growing all over the place. I could not move without stepping on one of them. I decided that all varieties of self-righteousness should be disposed of immediately, or they would take over the whole pathway.

Just thinking about all the work that needed to be done would not get the job finished unless I got started. I looked at the different things growing that I had never noticed before; wrong thinking, gluttony, lack of concern for others, an unloving spirit, selfishness, greed, and bitterness. It was hard for me to believe that these unattractive bushes had been growing in my pathway and I had not even realized it. It also surprised me when I found the bag of anger hidden under a big rock. I did not know I still had any anger around. It should have been disposed of a long time ago.

Then I stumbled over a large garbage bag that was marked treasures. Treasures? What would my treasures be doing in a garbage bag? I looked in and found an injustice done to me a long time ago, some unkind words that were said about me and many other similar things. I hardly considered these as treasures. I suppose anything you hang on to for a long time could be thought of as a treasure. And I had kept all of them. They would definitely have to be disposed of.

Working on the path was a never ending job. As soon as I cleaned one area and started on another section, the first one would start growing up again. I was not making much progress, and I still had not found my sandals.

Maybe it would help if I replanted something attractive; like a loving spirit in place an unloving spirit, or replacing a concern for others for a lack of concern. Trying to replace the unwanted things with something desirable was a big job. I had to keep going over the same area. The old bushes kept growing back, and the new plants needed to be watered and cared for.

What really got me behind was when I decided to help my husband with his path. He did not want my help but I thought he needed it. That was a big mistake - trying to help him clean up his pathway when mine needed so much done to it. I am not responsible for what is growing in his path anyway. That is his responsibility.

I finally reached the end of my path but it was a struggle. I did find my sandals and will try to keep up with them from now on. If the pathway stays cleared there won't be so many areas where I might lose them. The wisest decision is for me to keep a close watch for any unwanted growth. I can get at it right away before it chokes out the new plants.

I am so glad I found my sandals of peace. From now on, if I do misplace them, I will know where to start looking.

INTRODUCTION

This is an allegory - fantasy intertwined with truth. It is the writer's desire that you separate truth from fantasy. If you become aware of a lack of peace in your own life you may consider putting on each piece of your armor at the start of the day.

There are four main characters: the Bible teacher and three young women in her Bible class. As you become acquainted with them and their needs, you may identify similar needs in your own life.

Sections:

The Rusty Armor
The Sword of the Spirit
The Sandals of Peace
The Helmet of Salvation
The Breastplate of Righteousness
The Girdle of Truth
The Shield of Faith
The Preparation for the Battle
Dear Friend

THE RUSTY ARMOR

Let me introduce myself. My name is Maggie and I am the one who lost her sandals of peace. It all came about because a friend, Susan, invited me to go with her to a Bible Study. After unsuccessfully trying to get me there for several weeks, she called and said, "Maggie, tomorrow is the last class of the season. This series has been very helpful in giving me a better understanding of some important issues of life. I do wish you would come along. I feel this session could be meaningful to both of us."

From what I could see, Susan did not seem to need much help. If she thought the class would benefit her, maybe it would be helpful for me. Since this was the last class, I could give it a try without feeling obligated to attend more than one time.

The teacher was just starting the lesson as we arrived. "For the past several weeks we have been studying Ephesians. It clearly states how we should live, and it explains the advantages of living this way. We are told to put off the old life of turmoil and frustrations and put on a new and better life of peace and love. We also learned that God's mighty power is there to help us. It sounds like a wonderful life, doesn't it? Then, why is it so hard for us to live this way?"

She continued without waiting for an answer, "The last chapter speaks about an enemy that will try to make it impossible for us to experience this wonderful life of peace, love, and contentment. But, God has provided a way for us to be protected from this evil one. The first thing I do each morning is put on my armor," she said.

I leaned over to my friend Susan and asked, "What is she talking about, `her Armor'?"

"The Armor of God," Susan answered and pointed out the eleventh verse of the last chapter. "Put on the full armor of God, that you may be able to stand firm against the schemes of the devil."(NAS)

The teacher went on to say, "The reason I put on my armor every morning is for protection from the enemy".

It surprised me she had any enemies, from what Susan had been telling me about her.

Even though I had never heard of the Armor of God, that verse kept coming back to my mind throughout the rest of the lecture. I decided if the Bible teacher needed protection from the enemy, then surely I did, also.

There was no opportunity for me to ask the teacher how I could get a set of this Armor. She had to leave for an appointment immediately after class was over.

On my way home I stopped at the Book Store to see if they could help me.

The clerk said, "Yes, we do carry the whole set of Armor. Would you like for me to show it to you?"

"Yes, I would." I answered.

The first piece she showed me was the Girdle of Truth, whatever that means.

"Is the Armor just for ladies?" I asked.

"Oh no," she said, "it is for everyone. Why don't you try it on? It fits around your waist like a belt. In fact, some people call it the Belt of Truth."

Since I did not want to feel too confined wearing it, I asked to try the extra large.

"I'm sorry," she said, "but it only comes in small, medium and large."

"Well, bring me the largest one you have," I said.

She took me to a dressing room where I could try it on.

"It is tight," I told her, "but maybe I can wear it."

Next she brought in the Breastplate of Righteousness. Well, it was more uncomfortable than the girdle.

I asked her if we could bend it so it would fit better, but she said, "No."

She did bring me another one to try that was a little more comfortable.

I think the first one was made for a man. Men and women are shaped so differently that it is not surprising the first one did not fit.

It would have been easier to wear if I could have bent it a little. I tried, but it would not bend at all.

When I asked if she had any shoes, she said they came with the Armor. Fortunately, there were some sandals that fit. I'm glad I could get Sandals; they are so much more comfortable than plain shoes.

I put on the Breastplate and Girdle, thanked the clerk, picked up my old shoes, and started to leave.

She called me back to show me some other pieces of the Armor; the shield of Faith and the Sword of the Spirit.

I had seen the teacher with a Shield and a Sword but I thought she had them just because she was the teacher.

The saleslady said, "No, she does not have them just because she is the teacher. They are very important pieces of the Armor, and you definitely will need them."

Well, this was my first Shield or Sword. I started out the door and almost dropped the Shield when I tripped over the Sword.

I went back in and asked, "Why is it so important for me to carry this sword everywhere I go? I can see how the Shield could be of help but I do not understand why I need the Sword."

"You need the Sword of the Spirit to defend yourself

when you are attacked by the enemy. It is important that you learn how to use it."

She went on to say, "I'm sorry you almost fell down, but I'm glad you came back. "I had forgotten to ask you if you needed the Helmet of Salvation, or do you already have one? So many people in a Bible class already have the Helmet."

"I have only attended the class one time. I do remember something being mentioned about a helmet of salvation, but it was not clear to me that I needed it."

The saleslady explained that the rest of the Armor would not be any protection without the Helmet.

If it went with the armor I decided to get it, also. When I tried to pay her for it she said that the Helmet of salvation is a free gift to anyone who will meet the conditions.

"What are the conditions?" I asked.

"The book of instructions that comes with the Sword, says if you believe and trust in Jesus Christ you can receive the Helmet of Salvation. He is just waiting for you to invite Him into your life."

"How do I do that?" I asked.

"By prayer," she said, "Just tell Him you need Him to come into your life and take charge. If you ask, He will come in."

"I did not fully understand what it all meant, but I did as she suggested and received my Helmet of Salvation."

When I started to leave she showed me a holder on the Girdle that the Sword fit into, so I would not trip over it again. That worked out much better. I thanked her once more and left the store with the Helmet on my head and the Shield in my hand. I had on the Girdle of Truth with the Sword in the holder and the very uncomfortable Breastplate of Righteousness. I was also wearing my new Sandals of Peace.

There I was all decked out in my new and shining armor. I was pleased to have my very own set, even though I did not fully understand what I was being protected from.

One morning, as I was putting on my Armor, I noticed some rusty spots on the Shield of Faith. To be perfectly truthful, I had not been as faithful to put on the Armor each day as I had intended, so was not aware the Shield was in that condition.

I kept it right by the front door, readily available, but would often forget to take it. The Helmet of Salvation was like new, but the Breastplate of Righteousness was still very uncomfortable and the Girdle of Truth needed some repairs.

The Sword was the only piece of the Armor that came with any instructions and I had misplaced them.

Susan told me my Sword was supposed to be sharper than any other two-edged sword, but mine was not very sharp. Just sitting around with a Sword that needed sharpening, wearing that rusty Armor, waiting to be attacked by some unknown enemy, was not what I wanted to be doing.

I knew each piece of the Armor should be carefully examined and the necessary repairs made, but I did not know where to begin. I was beginning to be very frustrated with the whole situation. Maybe the Bible teacher would help me.

I got in touch with her and she agreed to meet with me and explain each piece of the Armor and how to care for it.

"Bring your Book of Instructions that came with the Sword," she said. "And bring all of your Armor."

I had not seen that Book since the day I brought it home. I finally located it on the table under a pile of magazines. Very seldom did I read the instructions that came with anything, so had not thought these were very important, either. But, the teacher was so insistent on having me bring it, maybe it is more important than I had realized.

That was when I missed my Sandals of Peace. Do you remember me telling you about finding them in the pile of garbage? I was so glad I found my sandals and could take them when I met with the teacher.

THE SWORD OF THE SPIRIT

Since I had found all the pieces of my Armor, I called the teacher and made plans to meet with her. "Be sure and bring your Book of Instructions that came with the sword," she reminded me. "We will be using it every time we meet."

When I told Susan that I was meeting with the teacher, she said, "I would like to learn how to care for my armor, also." Patricia, another friend from the class, also expressed an interest in going with us.

The first thing the teacher did was explain in detail about the Book of Instruction. Susan and Patricia knew all about the Book, but I didn't.

"This Book is the Holy Bible. It is the Word of God. We can read in II Peter 1:21 that God instructed men what to write. `For no prophecy was ever made by an act of human will, but men moved by the Holy Spirit spoke from God.' (NAS) It is the greatest Book ever written. It gives us instruction on how to live, offers comfort in our sorrow, advise for our problems and has an answer for our every need. It also points out our sinfulness and tells us what to do about it."

"Do you mean all of that is in the Bible?" I said.

"Yes it is, Maggie. The Bible reveals the truth about God and explains how we can spend eternity in Heaven with Him. It is the Book we will be using to teach you about caring for your Armor.

"The Sword of the Spirit, the Word of God, is a defensive weapon. This is the first piece of the armor we will be studying. Having God's Word firmly planted in our hearts helps us resist the attacker before he can start the battle. A good place to start is to see what the Bible has to say about itself. Susan, please read 2 Timothy 3:16-17."

"I'm using the Living Bible, is that all right?"

The teacher said that would be fine. She explained that although the Living Bible is not a translation, it is an accurate paraphrase which explains the Scripture in clear, simple ways, making it easier to understand.

"II Timothy 3:16-17, 'The whole Bible was given to us by inspiration from God and is useful to teach us what is true and to make us realize what is wrong in our lives; it straightens us out and helps us do what is right. It is God's way of making us well prepared at every point, fully equipped to do good to everyone.'" (TLB)

"Thank you, Susan, that explains how the Bible was written and that it is useful to teach us the truth."

"What does that mean, the Bible was given by inspiration from God?" I asked.

"Maggie, God often puts thoughts into our mind. His Holy Spirit exerted a supernatural influence upon the writers of the Bible. It really is God's Word for us, and not just the thoughts of men."

"Patricia, read II Samuel 23:2 and see what David said about the Lord speaking through him."

"The Lord spoke by me, and His Word was on my tongue." (NAS) Patricia said, "God also told David what to say, didn't he?"

"Yes, He did, Patricia, and that was in Old Testament times many years before Jesus was even born. Maggie, please read Hebrews 4:12."

I twisted nervously in my seat. Seeing my hesitation, the teacher said, "Susan will help you find it."

"For the Word of God is living and active and sharper than any two-edged sword, and piercing as far as the division of soul and spirit, of both joints and marrow, and able to judge the thoughts and intentions of the heart." (NAS)

Patricia said, "My Sword is not very sharp."

"Mine isn't either" I said. "Susan, I remember when you told me my Sword should be sharper than any two-edged sword, but I didn't know that was in the Bible."

"How can we sharpen our Swords?" Patricia asked.

"One way is to read the Bible daily and to memorize meaningful passages," she said.

"When Satan tempted Jesus, he quoted Scripture to Him.

Jesus answered back with Scripture. If we know the scriptures, we can use it to defend ourselves."

The teacher said to Patricia, "Do you spend much time reading the Word of God?"

"Not really, but I know I should."

"Yes, you should. In fact, we all should spend more time reading the Bible."

Susan said, "I try to read some portion of scripture each day, but sometimes I miss."

The teacher turned to me and said, "What about you, Maggie. Do you ever read the Bible?"

"Not very often," I said. I did not want to tell her that I never read the Bible. I didn't even have one until I got the Book of Instructions that came with the Armor.

She said, "I hope all three of you will develop the habit of daily reading God's Word. As you study, it is a good idea to write down one key verse on a 3 & 5 card to memorize. You will learn it faster if you carry the card with you, so you may refer to it throughout the day."

"Susan, please read II Timothy 2:15."

"Work hard so God can say to you, `Well done'. Be a good workman, one who does not need to be ashamed when God examines your work. Know what His Word says and means." (TLB)

"Remember to keep your Sword sharp, start each day by reading God's Word, meditating on it and applying what you read to your daily life."

"If you pay close attention to what it is saying, it will become more real to you. Your part is to claim the promises, obey the instructions, and apply the principles."

"Look at Ephesians 6:10-11. What are we told to do?"

I said, "The first verse says to be strong in the Lord. How does one get to be strong in the Lord.?"

"There are many places in the Bible that tell us how to do this. Psalms 138:3 says; `When I pray, You answer me and encourage me by giving me the strength I need.'(TLB) So one way is to ask for strength when we pray. He will give us the strength we need to handle whatever comes our way. As you read the Bible look for other verses that apply."

"In II Thessalonians 3:3, Paul told the church that the Lord is faithful and He will strengthen and protect them from the evil one."

"What are we told to do in Ephesians 6:11?" the teacher asked.

I said, "It says to put on the full Armor. That sounds

like it is up to us."

"That is exactly right. It is an act of our will. As we are studying the Armor, I want you to think of putting on each piece when you first wake up. Each day we should prayerfully ask the Holy Spirit for strength, guidance and to protect us from the evil one."

"I don't understand about the Holy Spirit. Asking a Spirit to guide me sounds kind of spooky," I said.

"Maggie, as we are learning to care for the Armor, I will explain some of what you missed in previous classes. By the time we finish, you should have a better understanding of what we are talking about.

"Susan, do you remember, in our first class we talked about how God's Spirit is with all of us who have received salvation?"

"Yes, I do. I'm sorry that Patricia and Maggie missed that first lesson because you explained that all who trusted in Christ were given the Holy Spirit and that His presence within us is God's guarantee that we belong to Him."

I had only attended the last class, but I think that Pat had been to a couple of classes before I came.

"There are two spirits that are active in our world today, the Holy Spirit and the unholy spirit," she said.

"Is the unholy spirit why we need the Armor for protection?" "That is exactly right, Susan. The unholy spirit is the evil one from whom we need to be protected. He is the enemy. That is why God provided the Armor for us.

"The Holy Spirit is the Spirit of God. He is also called Comforter, Helper, Spirit of Truth and several other names.

"Jesus told the disciples it was necessary for Him to go away so the Helper could come and be with them. He was talking about the Holy Spirit." (John 16:7-15)

"Did He?"

"Did He what, Maggie?"

"Did the Holy Spirit come like He said?"

"Yes, He did. There are many places in the Bible that tell us about the Holy Spirit. God wants us to have a life filled with peace and joy and to have fellowship with Him. When we have a right relationship with Him, it is much easier to have right relations with others.

The enemy wants just the opposite. That is why it is so important for us to be filled and controlled by the Holy Spirit, and to have on our Armor."

Look back at Ephesians 6, verses 14-17 and list the different parts of the armor.
1. Girdle of Truth
2. Breastplate of Righteousness
3. Sandals of Peace
4. Shield of Faith
5. Helmet of Salvation
6. Sword of the Spirit

"In different translations, these parts of the Armor have other names, but these are the names we will be using."

"They are not listed in the order a soldier would put them on. He would probably put the Sandals on first and then the Breastplate. The Girdle would be next as it holds the Breastplate in place and has a holder for the Sword."

"With the Breastplate, Girdle and Sword in place, the soldier would then put on his Helmet, pick up his shield and be ready for the battle."

"It will be much easier for us to lean over and put on the Sandals before we get all girded up, so we will put them on first."

THE SANDALS OF PEACE

"Footwear is very important to anyone going into battle. Ephesians 6:11-14 says three times to stand firm. You cannot stand firm without the proper shoes. Ephesians 6:15 says, `Wear shoes that are able to speed you on as you preach the Good News of Peace with God.' (TLB) These other passages also talk about this peace. Patricia, please read Ephesians 2:17."

"And He came and preached peace to you who were far away, and peace to those who were near." (NAS)

"Who is it that is preaching peace?" I asked.

"Paul is talking about Jesus Christ preaching peace."

"In John 14:27 Jesus said, `I am leaving you with a gift - peace of mind and heart! And the peace I give isn't fragile like the peace the world gives. So don't be troubled or afraid.' (TLB)

"Then, in Romans 5:1, Paul writes, `So now, since we have been made right in God's sight by faith in His promises, we can have real peace with Him because of what Jesus Christ, our Lord has done for us.' (TLB)

"God sent His Son into this world with the message of peace; peace with God, peace with others and peace of mind. Peace of mind is not available to us without peace with God. "Galatians 5:22 says, `But when the Holy Spirit controls our lives He will produce this kind of fruit in us: love, joy, peace, patience, kindness, goodness, faithfulness, gentleness and self-control.' (TLB)

"Are you experiencing these things in your life?" the teacher asked us.

Susan said, "Not really. I definitely need this peace that comes from God."

"Maybe there is something in your life keeping you from experiencing this kind of life. Could it be hidden anger or an unloving spirit? What about bitterness or selfishness. A lack of concern for others or a bad attitude can separate us from the Holy Spirit."

I interrupted the teacher, "You should be asking me instead ofSusan. She's so good. I am sure she is not bothered by any of those things."

"Maggie, let Susan decide for herself. By nature, we are all sinful. No matter how good we look to others, each of us has to make our own peace with God. No one can do it for us.

"Many times it is easier to make excuses for our attitudes and actions than to admit they are sins.

"In Psalms 32:3-5, David said, `There was a time when I wouldn't admit what a sinner I was. But my dishonesty made me miserable and filled my days with frustration. All day and all night Your hand was heavy on me. My strength evaporated like water on a sunny day until I finally admitted all my sins to You and stopped trying to hide them'" (TLB)

"David had definitely lost his peace, but found it when he admitted there was sin in his life.

"Patricia, would you read James 4;17?"

"Therefore, the one who knows the right thing to do and does not do it, to him it is sin.'" (NAS)

"That makes it very plain that knowing right from wrong is not enough," the teacher said.

"I was impressed when I heard a young minister's wife say, `I grew up in a Christian home where Christianity was not only taught, but lived. For some reason the truths that I heard never became a reality in my life. I was living a life of do's and don'ts, doing all the right things for all the wrong reasons. When I was able for the first time to see myself, I saw that I was impatient with my children, I lost my temper easily, I had a bad attitude, I didn't have an effective prayer life and on and on.' When she realized her life was not the way she wanted it to be, she did something about it. This was her prayer."

"Father, You see these areas of my life that are displeasing to You. I agree, they are sins. They are not mistakes but just plain old sins. I ask You to forgive me and I thank You that I am forgiven as you promised in Your Word. Take control of my life and make me the kind of person You want me to be."

It is as simple as 1-2-3.

1. Confess. Admit there is a sin problem.
2. Repent. Be willing to turn from it.
3. Accept forgiveness. Thank God that you are forgiven and finished with those sins.

Unless, of course, you keep on doing them, then you start over with step one."

"Romans 3:23 says that all of us have sinned, so let's examine our own heart right now. Is there unconfessed sin in our life that we need to deal with? If we ask, the Holy Spirit will bring to our minds the sins that we need to confess.

"If the Bible tells us not to do something, we can be sure it is sin, and we will lose our peace if we continue doing it. The time to take care of sin is now.

"I John 1:9 says; 'If we confess our sins, He is faithful and righteous to forgive us our sins and to cleanse us from all unrighteousness.'   (NAS)

"Do you have any questions about what we have been discussing?"

"I do," I said, "I have lots of questions. We started talking about the Sandals of Peace, and you began telling us about the Holy Spirit and confessing our sins.

Didn't we get off the subject?"

Susan said, "Maggie, it is all connected. Our peace directly relates to the Holy Spirit. We read in the Bible that when the Spirit of God controls our lives, He will give us peace."

"But what does the confession of sins have to do with the Holy Spirit?" I asked.

The teacher said, "God's Holy Spirit is not controlling our lives when we don't deal with areas of our life that we know are wrong. When that happens, the unholy spirit is in control. Which Spirit we listen to is our choice."

I was beginning to understand most of what they were saying. "How can I know which of my sins I need to confess? A bad attitude did not seem like sin until we began talking about it. I never thought of that as sin."

The teacher said, "It is hard to understand but we learn from the Word of God. John records Jesus telling the disciples what was going to happen to Him. In John 14:16, He told them He would send the Holy Spirit to be with them forever.

"Then in John 16:8, Jesus says, ʿAnd He, (the Holy Spirit) when He comes, will convict the world concerning sin and righteousness and judgment." (NAS)

"As the scripture tells us, it is the Holy Spirit who reveals the sin in our life, especially the sin of unbelief. When we ask to be made aware of our sins, we should confess whatever the Spirit of God brings to our mind.

"The way to be free from sin is to keep short accounts with God by confessing our sins as they occur, and then accept His forgiveness.

"Now are you ready to buckle up your Sandals of Peace?"

Patricia said, "I'm not ready. When you read that

the Holy Spirit convicts the world concerning sin, I knew that I could not fake it any longer. I do not have the whole Armor of God. I've never received the Helmet of Salvation."

"Patricia, you are so involved in the church. How have you missed receiving salvation? I feel like such a failure as your Bible teacher. I just assumed that you had accepted Christ because I saw you in the choir every Sunday and at the women's meetings. Please forgive me for being so insensitive to your need."

"Oh I do. It is difficult to explain and even harder for me to understand. My mother has taken me to church since I was a little girl and I've tried to live a Christian life. Many assumed, as you did, that I had received salvation. I did not understand the difference between knowing about Jesus and inviting Him to come in and take control. I believed He was the Son of God, but no one explained to me that I needed the Helmet of Salvation."

The teacher said, "Maybe you just did not hear what they were saying. Would you like to know how you how you can receive salvation? "

Patricia said, "Yes, I would."

THE HELMET OF SALVATION

"The Helmet is the most important piece of the Armor. No soldier would consider going into battle without his Helmet and we shouldn't either.

"Patricia, didn't you learn John 3:16 in Sunday School?"

"Oh yes, when I was a little girl."

"Then say it, as you learned it, except put your name instead of `the world'."

"<u>For God so loved the world</u> -sorry- <u>for God so loved</u> <u>Patricia that He gave His only begotten Son, that who-</u> <u>ever believes in Him should not perish, but have eter-</u> <u>nal life</u>."
(NAS)

"It is very important for you to understand that be-lieving in God is different from believing there is a God. 'Believing in' means trusting Him enough to be willing to turn our lives over to Him and ask Him to take con-trol. Many people believe there is a God, but have never accepted Him as the God of their life. They never read the Bible or try to be obedient to what the Bible says they should or should not do.

"There are others that try and live by the law of the land and never give a thought to God's laws. They feel if it is within the law, then it must be all right. They do not recognize their need for a relationship with the Cre-ator.

"Revelation 3:20 says: <u>'Behold, I stand at the door</u> <u>and knock; if anyone hears my voice and opens the</u> <u>door, I will come into him, and will dine with him, and</u> <u>he with Me</u>.' (NAS)

"Jesus Christ promised that when we invite Him into our life, to be our Savior, He will come in and es-tablish a personal relationship with us."

"Patricia, would you like to know God personally?"

"Oh yes, I would. How can I know Him in that way?"

"In John 14:6, Jesus said that He is the way, the truth and the life and that no one can come to the Father but through Him. So, just invite Jesus to come into your life and by faith accept the fact that He will come in because He said He would. Ask Him to forgive your sinfulness of unbelief and to take control of your life."

"Oh, I want to. May I do that now?"

"You surely may. The sooner you get this matter settled, the better it will be."

We all bowed our heads and Patricia said," Lord Jesus, I want You to come into my life. Please forgive me for my sinfulness of unbelief. For years, I have lived by my own standards of right and wrong and it has not been very successful. I'm ready now to try it Your way. Please come in and take control of my life. Make me the kind of person that You want me to be. Amen."

"Do you believe that Jesus Christ has come into your life and forgiven your sins?"

"Yes, I do."

"Then thank Him for doing what He promised."

"Heavenly Father, thank You for forgiving my sins and for giving me the Helmet of Salvation. I really love You for being so patient with me all the years I neglected You. Thank You for loving me and sending Your Son to die for my sins. I know I don't deserve it, which makes me even more grateful for what You have done for me. Thank You."

"Patricia, read Colossians 1:13-14 and see where you are now."

<u>"For He has rescued us out of darkness and gloom of Satan's kingdom and brought us into the kingdom of His dear Son, who bought our freedom with His blood and forgave us all our sins."</u> (TLB)

"It says that I am a part of God's kingdom. Isn't it wonderful to be rescued from Satan's kingdom? Now, I can be protected from this evil one." I'm ready to learn how to care for my Armor.

The teacher turned to Susan and me, "Are you both sure you have been rescued from Satan's kingdom and are a child of God?"

"I am," Susan said. "I accepted Christ as my Savior and Lord at church camp when I was a teenager."

I said, "I just invited Christ into my life a couple of months ago when the saleslady in the book store explained it to me."

But, I sure have learned more about it since you have been teaching us about how to care for the Armor. There was a lot that I did not understand, like recognizing what sin is, how to confess it, and about the Holy Spirit."

Susan said, "I have also gained a new understanding about confession. Since I became a Christian, I have tried to live a good life and just did not think of myself as a sinner. I see now that we are all sinners. Thank you for taking the time to teach us how to care for our Armor."

The teacher said, "I'm glad that I could be of help. Since we all now have a Helmet of Salvation, let's look at the next piece of the Armor that needs to be repaired."

THE BREASTPLATE OF RIGHTEOUSNESS

"When we became a child of God, we were brought into right relationship with Jesus Christ. This righteousness is only attainable through faith in Jesus Christ.

"However, we can't just <u>say</u> we are covered by the righteousness of Christ and then live anyway we want to. To live the kind of life that can win battles over the evil one, we must apply righteous principles to our daily lives.

"There are many advantages of having the Breastplate of Righteousness besides being protected from the fiery darts of the enemy. Patricia, please read Proverbs 10:3 and 15:29 which gives us two of the reasons for wearing it."

"<u>The Lord will not allow the righteous to hunger</u>"

and "The Lord is far from the wicked, but He hears the prayers of the righteous." (NAS)

"We find another reason for wearing the breastplate of righteousness in Proverbs 28:1. 'The wicked flee when no one is pursuing, but the righteous are as bold as a lion.'

"Maggie, read Philippians 3:8,9. Paul tells us where righteousness comes from."

"More than that, I count all things to be loss in view of the surpassing value of knowing Christ Jesus my Lord, for

whom I have suffered the loss of all things, and count them

but rubbish in order that I may gain Christ, and may be found in Him, not having a righteousness of my own derived from the Law, but that which is through faith in Christ, the righteousness which comes from God on the basis of faith." (NAS)

The teacher pointed out the righteousness of Christ comes to us from God. We receive it by faith. Then she asked me to read Ephesians 4:21-24.

Well, I read it to myself and tried to figure out what in the world it was talking about, the old self and the new self, taking off one and putting on the other one. It was confusing and sounded rather complicated, to say the least.

"Read it aloud, Maggie, so we can discuss it." the teacher said.

"Oh, I'm sorry, 'If indeed you have heard Him and have been taught in Him, just as truth is in Jesus, that, in reference to your former manner of life, you lay aside the old self, which is being corrupted in accordance with the lusts of deceit, and that you be renewed in the spirit of your mind, and put on the new self, which in the likeness of God has been created in righteousness and holiness of the truth.'"(NAS)

I said, "I don't understand what it is talking about—the old nature and the new nature. Does this have anything to do with becoming a Christian?"

"This is talking about how we should live after we become a Christian," she said. "It tells us that we should put aside our old evil nature and put on this new nature of Christ, like we would a piece of clothing.

"Let's look at it this way," she said. "We were born with an old sin nature. We do not have this sinful nature because we sin. We sin because our old nature is sinful. Now that we have received Christ, we do not have to listen to our old nature and let it control our lives. We now have a new righteous nature that is born of God.

"The old nature will sin anytime we let it. That is why we are told to put on this new nature. We choose which master we will serve. Do we wear the old nature or the new nature? It is for us to decide which master we will follow. Our old nature wants to please self and the new nature wants to please God.

"Before we are ready to put on the Breastplate of Righteousness we must have on the new nature that is born of God. How do we do this? We confess all known sin in our lives as the young minister's wife did. She invited Christ to come into her life and take charge."

I said, "Nobody is perfect. I know that I'm not. I probably will not ever be able to wear the Breastplate of Righteousness. I might as well forget it."

"Oh, Maggie, you can't forget it. You need the breastplate for protection from the fiery darts of the evil one. It tells you to put it on because you could be badly wounded without this protection. Even though you were brought into a right relation with Jesus Christ when you accepted Him as your Savior and Lord, it would be most uncomfortable for you to try to wear the Breastplate of Righteousness with unconfessed sin in your life."

"I'll have to remember that verse about confessing my sins and being forgiven. Isn't it in John somewhere?"

"Yes, it is, I John 1:9, Maggie. That is the solution to the sin in our lives. It is only through Jesus Christ that we can be set free from our old sin nature. Paul said no matter how hard he tried to do right, he just could not do it on his own. Neither can I and neither can you.

"I'm glad we have been given a new nature in Christ. Let's be sure we have it on so we can wear the Breastplate of Righteousness in comfort, with confidence. By faith, let's put it on."

THE GIRDLE OF TRUTH

"The Girdle of Truth fits around the waist like a belt. It holds the Breastplate in place and has a holder for the Sword, so it will be readily available."

Susan said," I remember the first time we met. You told us the Sword of the Spirit was a defensive weapon and that we could use it to resist the attacker."

"It can be, if we learn how to use it. One way to stand firm against the schemes of the devil is to learn what the Bible has to say about the Girdle of Truth."

"I'm tired of talking about the devil," I said. "Can't we talk about something else?"

Susan said, "I don't like talking about the devil either, Maggie. We need to learn about him so we can be protected from his attacks."

"That's right, Susan. None of us enjoy hearing about this evil one, but it does help to be informed," the teacher said. "If we know the truth there won't be confusion about what is truth and what is error."

"The most important truth is the gospel of Jesus Christ. In John 14:6 Jesus said that He is the way, the truth, and the life. In John 8:31-32, He told the believers, "If you abide in My word, then you are truly disciples of Mine; and you shall know the truth and the truth shall make you free."" (NAS)

I said, "If I apply the truth of the gospel to my life every day, it should make a difference in how I live."

"Yes it will, Maggie, in every area of your life as you mature and abide by what you have learned. The devil will continually try to steal the truth of the gospel from you. It is important to keep your armor on at all times."

Patricia said, "I think he stole the truth from me. That is why I did not have the Helmet of Salvation for so many years. It just had to be him that kept the truth from me."

The teacher said, "You are probably right, Patricia. You were hearing the gospel, but not receiving it. Becoming a child of God requires more than just knowing about Him. We must accept His Son as our Savior and invite Him to come in and be the Lord of our life."

Patricia said, "If the Girdle of Truth holds the armor together, then it is very important to know the truth and let it be our guiding force."

The teacher agreed, "It is necessary to know the difference between Truth and error so the evil one cannot confuse us with false doctrine."

"What is false doctrine?" I asked the teacher.

"Maggie, we should always look to God's Word for answers to our questions. Susan, please read 1 John 4:1,2 and the first part of verse 3 to see what the Bible says about false doctrine."

"Dearly beloved friends, don't always believe everything you hear just because someone says it is a message from God: test it first to see if it really is. For there are many false teachers around, and the way to find out if their message is from the Holy Spirit is to ask: Does it really agree that Jesus Christ, God's Son, actually became man with a human body? If so, then the message is from God. If not, the message is not from God but one who is against Christ." (TLB)

"In Ephesians 4 we also learn that as we become mature in our faith, we won't be changing our minds about what we believe. Clever lies won't even sound like truth."

Patricia said, "Does the truth of the Gospel have anything to do with not telling a lie?"

"Being truthful is giving out right information. If you tell a lie then you are not giving right information. It is the same with the Gospel. If someone is teaching wrong doctrine, the Bible tells us to avoid them. In John 4:24, Jesus said, `God is Spirit, and those who worship Him must worship in Spirit and truth.'"(NAS)

Patricia said, "Reading and meditating on the Word of God each day should help us to become established in the truth of the Gospel. Then we can't be fooled so easily."

The teacher said," Romans 12;3, warns us not to think more highly of ourselves than we ought. Even if we regularly study God's Word, we should not think we know it all. A guide to our ability is how well we have learned to distinguish between right and wrong, truth and error.

"Maggie, please read Ephesians 4:25."

"Therefore, laying aside falsehood, speak truth, each one of you, with his neighbor, for we are members of one another."

"The Gospel of Truth does make a difference in how we live. John says, `I have no greater joy than this, to hear of my children walking in the truth' III John 1:3 (NAS) By being truthful with others, they were living out the truth of the Gospel.

"We now have on our Helmet of Salvation, Sandals of Peace, Breastplate of Righteousness and wearing our Girdle of Truth. With the Sword of the Spirit at our side, it should not be too difficult to walk in truth after we pick up the last piece of Armor, our Shield of Faith."

THE SHIELD OF FAITH

I said to the teacher, "Now that we have on all of our armor, are we protected from the evil one?"

"Not without your Shield of Faith," she answered.

"About that shield," I said, "do you think that I could turn mine in and get another one? Besides being rusty, it is so small. Susan's is much larger than mine. If I had a larger shield I might remember to use it."

Patricia said, "My shield is small, also."

The teacher said, "It is possible that later you will receive a larger Shield of Faith. For now you must use the one you have. Of course, you can always ask for a larger one. The apostles did in Luke 17:5 and in verse 6 Jesus gave them an answer. Patricia, would you read that passage?"

"And the apostles said to the Lord, 'Increase our faith!' And the Lord said, 'If you had faith like a mustard seed, you could say to this mulberry tree, be uprooted and be planted in the sea; and it would obey you.'"(NAS)

"A mustard seed is very small," Patricia said. "It sounds like Jesus was telling them that even a little faith was all they needed. Maybe I should learn to use the Shield of Faith that I have, instead of asking for a larger one."

"I think that is a wise decision," the teacher said. "Maggie, how do you feel about it?"

"I don't think I have any other choice. I'm not even sure what faith is, anyway. Could you explain it to me?"

"I can try," the teacher said, "The dictionary describes faith as 'complete trust or confidence in anything believed'. You exercise your faith each day, without realizing it. You would not sit down in a chair if you did not have faith that it would hold the weight of your body and not break. When you turn on the tap to get a glass of water, you have faith that water will come out and be safe to drink."

"I often travel by air, so it requires me to have faith in the airline companies and the pilot. Without faith, I would never hand my luggage to a man standing on the street and give the ticket (that I had paid a lot of money for) to a man standing behind a counter, then go to another part of the building, get on an airplane that (in my estimation) is too big to even get off the ground, and expect it to fly me across the United States. That takes real faith."

"I believe the chair will hold me, that the water company is providing water safe enough for drinking and that I will arrive safely at my destination."

"Even though I have faith, there is no guarantee things will turn out the way I believe. Chairs break down, water does get polluted and planes do crash. This is not the kind of faith we are going to be learning about.

"The only faith that can win battles over the evil one is faith placed in Jesus Christ.

"Jesus said, 'I am the way, and the truth, and the life; no one comes to the Father, but through me.'" John 14:6 (NAS)

Patricia said, "You quoted that scripture when you were explaining how I could receive my Helmet of Salvation."

"Yes, I did. It was by faith that you believed Him to be the Son of God, who came to this earth and died for your sins. Then He rose from the dead and was bodily taken to heaven to be with God forever."

The teacher continued, "Faith is very important. Without it we would not have received the Helmet of Salvation. The Word of God is trustworthy."

I said, "I used my Shield of Faith when I accepted Jesus as my Savior. Evidently, I have not been using it in other areas of my life or my Shield would not have rusted."

"Maggie, you are beginning to understand. In addition to what Jesus said about being the way, the truth and the life, He also said: 'Therefore, do not be anxious for tomorrow; for tomorrow will care for itself. Each day has enough troubles of its own.'" Matthew 6:34 (NAS)

"In the previous verses Jesus tells the disciples that it does not do any good to worry. He says that the Heavenly Father knows what they need before they ask."

"I didn't know Jesus told us not to worry about tomorrow," I said. "I think worry may be the main reason that I lost my Sandals of Peace."

"You are probably right, Maggie. Worry can cause us to lose our peace. This is one of the ways the evil one gets to us."

"If I worry, does that mean that I'm not using my Shield of Faith?" I asked the teacher.

"Yes, it does. In John 14:1, Jesus said, 'Let not your heart be troubled; believe in God, believe also in me.'"(NAS)

"Jesus is saying to have faith in God and in Him,

also. To believe in someone means that you trust them. We can trust God because He is trustworthy. The chair is not always trustworthy to hold us without breaking; the water company is not always trustworthy to give us clean water; and airplanes are not always trustworthy to get us where we want to go. But as the Psalmist says, 'Forever, O Lord, Your Word stands firm in the heavens. Your faithfulness extends to every generation, like the earth You created; it endures by Your decree, for everything serves Your plans.'" Psalms 119:89-90 (TLB)

"Forever is a long time," I said. "There sure are many things in the Bible I never heard of. It is very difficult to have faith in what I don't know about."

"As you sharpen your Sword and become more familiar with the Scriptures, you will find many other instructions of Jesus that can be very beneficial if you abide by them," the teacher said. "The Bible is like a well. We can continually find refreshment as we drink from it. This well will never run dry, because there is always more available. However, we will run dry if we don't avail ourselves of this Living Water."

I said, "I don't understand what you are talking about, the Bible being like a well that we are to drink."

"I'm sorry, Maggie. Sometimes, people who have been a Christian for a long time make statements that are hard for a new believer to understand. I'll try to keep it simple from now on."

Patricia said, "I understand what you are saying. When I read the Bible before I received salvation, I was not refreshed by it. Since I have accepted Christ, the Bible is becoming more alive, and I understand it better."

"That is a very good point, Patricia. I'm glad you brought it out," the teacher said. "Yes, you do have to be a believer for the Bible to be meaningful and alive."

"My Shield of Faith was not useful then, either," Patricia said, "even the verses about faith that I memorized in Sunday School had no significance to me. Now that I have received salvation, I'm sure they will have more meaning."

"Yes, they will because it is the Spirit of God that teaches us the meaning of the Scriptures. Before you became a child of God, you did not have the Holy Spirit living in you, but now you do."

Patricia said to the teacher, "Thank you for explaining that to me. I am gradually understanding how to apply the Word of God to my life. It must be God's Spirit that is teaching me the truth."

"And it is by faith that you can accept this truth," the teacher said.

"I still don't understand where faith comes from," I said.

"Maggie, as I have said before, the Bible has all the answers to your questions. I have been spoon feeding the Word of God to the three of you. Now, it is time for you to start feeding yourself. Look up Romans 10:17 and 12:3 to see what the Spirit of God will teach each of you from the Word."

"Romans 10:17 says that faith comes from hearing the Word of God," I said. "For us to have faith, does that mean that someone has to read the Bible to us?"

"It does say that we receive faith by hearing the Word of God. The people in Paul's time did not have a Bible to read, like we do. Hearing someone read the scriptures was the only access they had to it. Now that we have the Word of God recorded, we can hear by reading it for ourselves."

Susan said, "I learn more when reading it myself than listening to someone else read it. I know that my faith has grown through reading God's Word."

"What did you learn from Romans 12:3?"

Patricia said, "That verse tells us to be honest in our estimate of ourselves."

"What does it say about faith?" the teacher asked.

"It says that God has given some faith to each of us."

"Maggie, now can you answer your question about where faith comes from?"

"The two scriptures we read indicate that faith is a gift from God and is also received by reading or hearing His Word," I answered.

"A gift is never ours until we accept it, and will not be useful until we begin to use it. When we were learning how to care for the Sword, I suggested that you start each day by reading God's Word, meditating on it and applying what you read to your daily life. Victory over the evil one will not be ours until these principles affect the way we live."

Susan said, "As I read my Bible, I began to underline faith each time I came across it, and was surprised at how many times it appeared. It seems to me that every area of our life is affected by faith."

The teacher said, "I feel that way too, Susan and you will find scriptures to verify this fact as you study God's Word. These are some verses to start with as you begin your own personal Bible study. Write down the key thought in each verse. If you have any questions, we can discuss them at a later time."

1. James 1:5,6

2. Romans 14:23

3. 2 Corinthians 5:7

4. Galatians 3:11

5. Ephesians 2:8

6. Ephesians 3:17

7. Hebrews 11:6

"God is on our side in this spiritual battle, but it is our responsibility to appropriate what we are learning. It does not do any good to have many facts stored in our head if they do not affect the way we live. It can even be harmful, because knowing what is right and not doing it is sin. Our security comes from having faith in Jesus Christ and abiding in His Word."

"We should stop right now and thank God for giving us this wonderful gift of faith," I said.

"Maggie, that is an excellent idea. Would you lead us in a prayer of thanksgiving?"

"Me? Pray out loud? I don't know how to pray. I meant for you to pray," I said.

"All right, I will. But, each one of you pray silently while I lead us in a prayer. "Psalms 92:1 says, 'It is good to give thanks to the Lord and to sing praises to His Name,' she said and then prayed this prayer.

"Heavenly Father, Thank you for the faith You have given each of us. We know by reading Your Word that salvation comes to us through faith in Jesus Christ, who died on the cross for our sins. When we accepted Him as our Lord and Savior, He came to dwell in us. It is by faith that we believe this, and can look forward to spending eternity in Heaven with You. Thank You for faith."

PREPARATION FOR THE BATTLE

"Although our main purpose of putting on the armor is for protection from the enemy, the emphasis should always be on the protector, not on the enemy. Our final session started with the same passage the teacher read the time I attended the class. `Finally, be strong in the Lord, and the strength of His might. Put on the full armor of God, that you may be able to stand firm against the schemes of the devil.' Ephesians 6:10-11 (NAS)

"The armor of God is special because it is OF GOD," she said. "Without God's Spirit and guidance it would be like Goliath's armor. He had a bronze helmet; was clothed in a bronze scale-armor, bronze greaves on his legs, a bronze javelin and a spear with an iron head. By man's standard, he was well protected, but was no match for one small boy armed with God's Spirit.

"David said even though Goliath was coming at him with a sword, spear and javelin, he was coming in the name of the Lord, so all the earth may know there is a God of Israel."

The teacher continued, "Without the Armor of God, we are no match for the devil's cunning and crafty ways. Our only hope of winning the battles that are continually being waged against us is to have on the full Armor of God.

Patricia said, "I do not know much about the devil."

"That's true, Patricia, we have not spent much time talking about this evil one. It is important that we have enough information to recognize there is a dangerous enemy, waiting for an opportunity to attack us. He has many names: Devil, Adversary, Satan, the Evil One, Ruler of Demons and Murderer. There are many other names for him, but these are the most familiar.

"To gain some insight as to who we are dealing with, let's look in the Word of God and write down what the Holy Spirit teaches us."

1. Matthew 4:1-11

2. 1 Peter 5:8-9

3. 2 Corinthians 11:14

4. John 8:44

5. 1 Thessalonians 2:18

"Wow! I had no idea the enemy was anything like that. No wonder we need protection. It's really scary," I said.

"Maggie, you are right. It is scary. That is why we should take advantage of all protection available to us. We cannot just write Satan off as some evil force out there some where. We must recognize that he is real and can attack us at any time."

Patricia said, "Wearing the Armor of God became important to me when I read that the devil is prowling around looking for someone to devour."

"It should be important to every child of God."

"Ephesians 6:12 says, `For our struggle is not against flesh and blood but against the rulers, against the powers, against the world forces of darkness and against the spiritual forces of wickedness in heavenly places.'" (NAS)

Susan said, "It sounds like Satan has a well orga-
nized army. We need to understand how to deal with
these powerful forces."

"Yes, we do, Susan. But the Scripture tells us the
Son of God came that He might destroy the works of
the devil." (1 John 3:8)

"How did He do that?" I asked.

"In Hebrews 2:14, we learn that through the death
of Jesus Christ the devil was rendered powerless because Jesus conquered death." The teacher continued,
"The same power that dealt the defeating blow to this
evil one, resides in us, which gives us a decided advantage.

"Paul does warn the Christians not to give the devil
any opportunity, and he gives instructions on how to
live so we won't be so vulnerable."

"Ephesians 4:25-32 list at least ten things he tells
them they should or should not do."

_____
_____
_____
_____.

The whole Bible deals with the way God wants His
children to live."

The Spirit of God living in us is our greatest weapon.
For the Holy Spirit to be in control, we should not have
any unconfessed sin in our life. This sin will short cir-
cuit the power of the Holy Spirit."

Patricia said, "One of the things on my list from
that Scripture is not to grieve the Holy Spirit. Exactly,
what does that mean?"

"Just what we have been talking about, Patricia.
Unconfessed sin in our life grieves the Holy Spirit," the

teacher said.

Susan said, "I think it means not to just do what we want without even thinking about what God wants us to do."

"That, too," she said, "We still have our will, and when the old sinful nature is in control, we will always do what we want without even thinking about what God wants."

"We can't blame the devil when we are messing up on our own, can we?" I said.

"I think all three of you are right. If we let our old nature take over, there is no need for any evil force to do a special work. Of course, the devil will always be glad to help us think up excuses for our actions, instead of admitting them as sin."

Susan said, "That is what happened to David, isn't it? He said that he was miserable, until he finally admitted all of his sins to God."

"I remember reading that in Psalms when we were getting ready to put on our Sandals of Peace." Patricia said, "One way Satan attacks us is by stealing our peace. David did not have any peace until he confessed his sins."

"That's right, Patricia. That is why it is so important that we do not have any unconfessed sin in our life. Do you remember the three steps to take when you recognize things that need to removed?"

She said, "I remember two of them; admit there is sin and stop doing it. I don't remember the third one."

"The last one is to accept forgiveness and thank God that He has forgiven you," the teacher said. "To stay on the winning side of the battle, have an Armor check first thing each morning."

"I have my Sandals of Peace ready to put on," I said.

"Then put them on. This peace that comes from God

is one thing Satan will never be able to counterfeit.

"How about your Swords? Have you been reading God's Word and memorizing meaningful passages.? If you are not doing this regularly, your Sword will not be very sharp.

"Be sure to check your Breastplate of Righteousness for unconfessed sins you may have overlooked. You know what to do. Confess your sin and accept forgiveness.

"Is the truth of the gospel becoming more real to you? This holds the Armor together. What about truthfulness in other areas of your life?"

I said, "Two things on my list of things that Paul said to do were lay aside falsehood and speak truth,"

"The Girdle of Truth holds the Shield of Faith in place. Are you wearing it faithfully?"

Susan said, "It is much easier to have faith when all is going well and my plans are working out to suit me. It's a different story when trouble comes. Most of the time, I don't realize that I am not using my Shield for protection, until the battle is well on it's way."

The teacher said, "We are prime targets for the evil one to attack us when we are not using any piece of the Armor." Even though we are wearing the Helmet of Salvation, it is still our responsibility to protect our mind. We should be careful what we allow to invade our thoughts."

Patricia said, "Do you mean, like television?"

"Television is one thing we must guard against. It is our responsibility to be cautious about what we see and hear. Are you bothered by the immoral acts and filthy language as much as you used to be? Our purpose here on earth is to glorify God. Spending hours in front of a television set is not fulfilling that purpose."

"What are some other things we should avoid to protect our mind?"

Susan said, "Listening to gossip, and then repeating it. The Bible certainly condemns that."

"I think some of the music on the radio is unhealthy," Patricia said.

"What are we going to do if we can't look at TV, or listen to music on the radio?" I said. "A person can't just read the Bible all the time."

"Maggie, all television is not bad, neither is all radio.

The teacher went on to say," It is most important to remember to beware of the enemy. Don't take anything from the devil without putting up a fight."

"Use your Sword of the Spirit (the Word of God),"

"Hold up your Shield of Faith,"

"Tighten up your Belt of Truth."

"You have on your Helmet of Salvation,"

"Buckle up your Sandals of Peace,"

"Be sure that you do not have any holes in your Breastplate of Righteousness."

"As I have reminded you before, put on your armor each morning. With your Armor, you can be protected.

"It sounds like we are getting ready for a battle, and we are. There definitely is a war going on and we want to be prepared, don't we?" the teacher said to us.

Susan said, "I certainly do."

Patricia and I both agreed.

All three of us thanked the teacher for taking the time to show us how to care for our Armor.

Now it was time to start living what we had been learning. Trying to hold on to my Sandals of Peace turned out to be more of a problem than I thought it would be.

I found out the other girls were having to deal with the same situation. Both of them had lost their peace and could not figure out what had caused it.

I received a letter from Patricia which may be an explanation of my problem as well as hers.

Dear Maggie,

I was so sorry to hear of your loss. The same thing happened to me last week. I, too, lost my peace.

At least that is what I thought until I found out it was not lost, but had been stolen. Can you believe someone would actually steal another person's peace?

Well it happened, and I found out who did it. I knew about this fellow because I have had trouble with him before. He must live near by, because he is always hanging around my house, trying to get in.

He lies and steals and is not someone I want around, mainly because he cannot be trusted.

I found out that he had taken my peace when I caught him in my house, trying to get out the door with my joy.

"You put that down," I demanded. "How did you get in.? I thought the doors were locked and bolted to keep you out."

"Well, they weren't. One door was not quite closed and I just walked in."

It must have happened when I came in the house with my arms full of packages. Those large bags of frustration I was bringing in from the car probably caused me to be careless about locking and bolting the door.

"Did you steal my peace?" I asked.

"No ma'am, I did not?" he said.

"Yes, you did! Now you bring it right back. That was a gift to me from God, and I want it back, now. Is that clear?"

"O K, O K, I'll bring it back. Now get off my back."

"I'll get off your back when you leave me alone. You

have no right to even be in here, and I want you out, now."

"Knock it off, lady. I'm leaving."

"Good," I said and meant it.

I hope that sharing my experience might help you get back your peace. It was probably stolen, too.

We should not have to take a lot of abuse from any thief because greater is He that is in us than he that is in the world. It would be nice if we did not have to always be so careful and could just get rid of that fellow for good, but I don't know how to do that.

I don't want to take a chance of him slipping in again so I'm keeping my doors locked and bolted from now on. I suggest you do the same.

I also plan to consistently wear my Armor. It is so easy to forget to put it on when everything is going good.

Do let me know if you find your peace. By the way, is your joy missing, also? If it is, I hope you find it soon.

Much love to you,
Patricia

P.S. I'm also writing to Susan. I understand that she, too, lost her peace.

Jesus said, "The thief comes only to steal, and kill and destroy; I came that they might have life and might have it abundantly." John 10:10 (NAS)

About the Authors

Lois Tumblin Eger was a native of Florida. Her mother was a direct descendant of Benjamin Harrison, a co-signer of the Declaration of Independence, and the grandfather of William Henry Harrison, the 23rd President of the United States. Lois and her husband Leroy, traveled the United States and many foreign countries during the last 30 years of her life as staff members for Campus Crusade for Christ. During those years Lois became a prolific writer of wit and wisdom. *Pathway to Peace* is an anthology of her writings and her wisdom as well as a brief biography composed from interviews with Lois, family and friends written by Keith Money. It is a legacy that will touch the hearts of those who read her stories, allegories and poetry.

Keith Money lives with his wife Susan in Lake Mary, Florida. He has two daughters Jamey and Ashley. He is a native of North Carolina and is a graduate of Wingate University, N.C., where he received a degree in Religious Studies and History. He has completed graduate work at Southeastern Baptist Theological Seminary and the University of Chicago. He is an ordained minister in the Southern Baptist Church and an executive in the high technology industry.